CW00684689

COMMERCIALIZE

Praise for *Commercialize*

"All too often, companies misdiagnose the poor performance of scalable, packaged services as a "product" or "sales" problem. Commercialize makes it very clear that it is actually a strategy problem—and provides a clear blueprint for surmounting it."

TOM MONAHAN,
CHIEF EXECUTIVE OFFICER, HEIDRICK & STRUGGLES

"Every professional services leader aspires to bring more consistent, predictable growth to their firms. One of the most powerful ways to do that is to introduce productized offerings to the firm's revenue mix—but pulling this off successfully is far easier said than done. Too often, firms pour valuable resources into developing compelling products for their clients only to see them stumble out of the gates because the sales motion required for products is misaligned with the firm's legacy go-to-market approach. In this excellent follow-on book to *Productize* and *Fearless*, Eisha Armstrong provides the definitive road map firm leaders need to avoid this painful outcome and put their organizations on a path to sustainable, predictable revenue."

MATTHEW DIXON,
FOUNDING PARTNER OF DCM INSIGHTS AND WALL STREET
JOURNAL-BESTSELLING CO-AUTHOR OF THE ACTIVATOR ADVANTAGE,
THE CHALLENGER SALE AND THE JOLT EFFECT.

"Eisha Armstrong's first book *Productize* was a game changer for many professional services firms to help them move from pure services to more packaged offers that can drive growth at scale. *Commercialize* provides a perfect follow-up addition to tackle the equally difficult challenge of engineering a commercial strategy and structure that allows you to take packaged service offerings to market. Great packaged products and services are only half the battle. This book provides you with the commercial gameplan to win the second part of that battle."

CHRISTOFFER ELLEHUUS,
CHIEF EXECUTIVE OFFICER, MINDGYM

"Selling products is a tempting but tricky endeavor for professional services firms used to positioning the expertise locked inside their people's heads. *Commercialize* offers firm leaders a compelling roadmap to scale high-margin products, born out of years of careful observation and insightful course correction, spelled out in detailed fashion by Armstrong."

TED MCKENNA,
CO-AUTHOR OF THE JOLT EFFECT: HOW HIGH
PERFORMERS OVERCOME CUSTOMER INDECISION

"Two chapters into this book, I texted my co-founder telling him to drop everything and read it. The authors' insights are spot-on, offering tremendous value in navigating the complexities of productization. This is a must-read for any service business looking to evolve."

ALEXANDER YASTREBENETSKY,
CHIEF EXECUTIVE OFFICER, INFOTRUST

"I've seen dozens of consultancies attempt to build and sell products, but the vast majority fail. *Commercialize* is an invaluable resource for any professional services firm seeking to avoid failure. Armstrong, Boldt, and Gillispie have masterfully distilled years of experience and countless case studies into a practical, actionable guide. Their insights on market understanding, pricing strategies, and building effective go-to-market capabilities are profound and practical.

The authors' approach is refreshingly honest, acknowledging the challenges and pitfalls that many firms face when transitioning from services to products. They offer clear, step-by-step advice for each stage of the commercialization process, from initial concept to scaling a mature product.

What sets this book apart is its deep understanding of the unique cultural and operational challenges that service firms face when productizing. The authors don't just tell you what to do; they show you how to overcome internal resistance, align incentives, and foster the mindset shifts necessary for success.

Commercialize is more than just a book; it's a roadmap for transformation that will help professional services firms thrive in an increasingly product-driven world."

JOE O'MAHONEY,
PROFESSOR OF CONSULTING, CARDIFF UNIVERSITY AND AUTHOR OF
GROWTH: BUILDING A CONSULTANCY IN THE DIGITAL AGE

Commercialize: How to Monetize, Sell, and Market Productized Offerings in Professional Services

Copyright © 2024 by Eisha Armstrong

All rights reserved.

No part of this book may be used, reproduced or stored in a retrieval system, or transmitted in any form or by any means – electronic, mechanical, photocopying, recording or otherwise – without the express permission of the publisher.

Published by Vecteris
www.vecteris.com

First Edition

Book Cover Design by ebooklaunch.com

Paperback ISBN: 978-1-7369296-3-6
Hardcover ISBN: 978-1-7369296-5-0
Ebook ISBN: 978-1-7369296-4-3
Audiobook ISBN: 978-1-7369296-6-7

Printed in the United States of America

COMMERCIALIZE

HOW TO MONETIZE, SELL, AND MARKET PRODUCTIZED OFFERINGS IN PROFESSIONAL SERVICES

by
Eisha Armstrong
with
Jason Boldt and Sean Gillispie

To Kate,
the most courageous person I know

CONTENTS

AUTHORS' NOTE

Over the last six years, we talked to hundreds of professional services leaders about transforming their organizations to pursue a strategy of "productization" (standardizing and often tech-enabling their services to scale). The stories you'll read in this book came out of those conversations and from a focused set of qualitative interviews we conducted in 2023.

Marketing and selling customized services are very different from the go-to-market motions required to successfully market and sell standardized services or products. Moreover, there are no tried-and-true playbooks for successful commercialization of products or productized services *in an organization that is purpose-built to sell customized services*. The individuals who develop and execute the go-to-market strategy for productized services are forging new ground and often make mistakes along the way. If you are struggling to market and sell your organization's new solutions and products, you are not alone.

The individuals developing and executing the go-to-market strategy for new productized services are often new to the organization or "wired differently" from everyone else. One product leader, responsible for the launch of her firm's first productized service, shared with us:

> *"Being one of the only product-minded people at my firm is lonely and often thankless. It is a combination of exhaustion, a lack of support, and deeper issues of mistrust coupled with high workload, a lack of autonomy, and others questioning your expertise."*

In this book, you will learn from other leaders' successes, struggles, and failures to learn how to successfully go to market with productized solutions and products. Some stories have been told without alteration, using real names and circumstances, and always with that person's permission. In other cases, we have anonymized and changed details to disguise the source and the organization.

We are grateful to all the leaders who so generously shared their experiences with us. We hope you will see your own experiences reflected in those we share, and they will give you the wisdom and courage you need to launch boldly and realize the full commercial potential of your offerings.

PREFACE

When I wrote my first book, *Productize,* in 2020, several forces were driving the interest in productizing* professional services:

1. COVID-19 drove digitization of delivery of professional services.

2. A significant increase in private equity investment in professional services focused effort on scaling and improving gross margins.

3. Across all industries, companies were creating digital businesses to stay economically viable.

I had no idea what was around the corner.

At the time of this writing, discussion about how artificial intelligence (AI) will disrupt the professional services industry has reached a fever pitch. And the excitement is warranted.

For example, the National Bureau of Economic Research recently looked at estimates of time and labor across seventeen different industries and found that the professional services industry has the highest amount of work—41 percent—that can be automated using generative AI[1]. Professional services leaders across all domains such as legal, management consulting, accounting, architecture, engineering, and marketing are racing to adopt AI to improve the speed and quality of research, analysis, and creation of their core knowledge work. They are

---

*   Using digital technology to scale services or create new offerings.

investing significant amounts of money to not just improve efficiency and scale but also to solve new client problems.

The CEO of a global consulting firm recently told me:

> *"It is the Wild, Wild West right now. But I know, with certainty, AI will be a revolutionary change, not an evolutionary change, for professional services firms."*

Generative AI forces professional services leaders to fundamentally rethink how they create value. And turning services organizations into solutions organizations that embrace both human expertise and technology is hard work.

While I am not an expert in AI, I am an expert in the capabilities needed to ensure that the investments services organizations are making in AI pay off. At my firm, Vecteris, we call these capabilities "productization" capabilities, and our mission is to help services organizations use technology to standardize, scale, and ultimately transform an industry that, until very recently, was relatively isolated from technological disruption.

I can confidently say that AI is already reshaping the professional services industry in many exciting ways, but the most exciting of all is as a **catalyst to develop new services and solutions.**

The most forward-thinking professional services leaders realize that AI allows them to solve new problems for customers. This is not only because AI frees up the time and information to spot new opportunities but also because AI invites leaders to rethink their business models. A change of this magnitude is a great opportunity to develop new offerings and serve new users or markets.

Consider the example of Katie Trauth Taylor, the CEO and founder of a marketing agency, Untold Content. Untold delivered two kinds of professional services: content strategy and creation for lean fast-growth start-ups innovating in technical fields and innovation communication training for scientists, technologists, and clinicians within Fortune 500 brands. The goal? To streamline communications in these demanding fields so that innovative ideas can be communicated with clarity and impact. Untold was an early adopter of GenAI and realized that it would significantly disrupt a key line of business. So, using generative AI and Untold's proprietary expertise, they created Narratize[2], a product that optimizes communication workflows for marketing, product, and R&D functions. This was a more radical shift. Untold was acquired by Narratize in 2023, Generative AI's breakout year. Their staff is now fully focused on delivering an AI-enabled digital product and experience to enterprise customers.

But developing and launching new solution opportunities is not a natural skill set for many of our employees. Leaders need to get two things right to succeed:

1. Developing the idea
2. Commercializing the idea

And, for professional services organizations, **commercializing new ideas is the most significant stall point.** Unfortunately, it's a failure story we see far too often. An organization conceives of, designs, and develops a promising, market-validated idea, but it does not sell.

There are many resources on how to develop new solutions and products. And there's a lot out there about how to sell successfully. But there's not a lot of information about how traditional B2B services organizations can successfully commercialize, or go to market, with more productized offerings. Successful commercialization is more than just marketing campaigns and training your sellers. It includes selecting your target markets, the pricing, the packaging, the messaging, and selecting the right sales channels. In a professional services firm, these go-to-market motions are often immature because the go-to-market has typically been about diagnosing client needs and estimating the time and materials needed to solve a particular client's need.

Even if I'm wrong and AI does not transform the professional services industry, I hope you'll agree that building the capabilities to successfully commercialize new ideas is an incredibly worthy endeavor.

—Eisha Tierney Armstrong
May 2024

CHAPTER 1
GREAT PRODUCT, FAILED LAUNCH

In 2016, the leadership team at TalentTether*, a global provider of outplacement services, launched a significant effort to productize their offerings. They had several goals: diversify their revenue, meet new customer needs, and to scale their growth. They saw how technological advancements, regulatory changes, and demographic changes were transforming the labor market and forecasted there would be new demand for reskilling workers and scaling their traditional outplacement services.

Over the next five years, they executed an ambitious plan to develop new products and digitize the delivery of existing services.

When they started, their go-to-market approach was very traditional. Consultants (i.e., sellers) were assigned geographic territories and called upon businesses in those territories to land new clients and retain and grow existing clients. The consultants were responsible for prospecting and had discretion on how best to hit their goals. There was little marketing.

Five years later, their go-to-market strategy and motions had completely evolved to support the productization strategy. Firm lead-

---

*   Pseudonym

ers admit their journey was not without mistakes, and they evolved through a process of trial and error.

For example, they initially placed lower cost, lower converting products that solved an entirely different customer problem into the same white-glove, consultative sales channel that traditionally sold outplacement and executive coaching services. When the products did not sell as expected, the firm introduced premium incentives for the products, but the large incentives reduced the profitability because of the higher customer acquisition costs.

Then, they kept adding more new products, eventually expanding the portfolio so substantially that just training the sales teams on the new products required four days a week for two months out of the year.

They also experimented with selling products and productized services online to small- to medium-sized businesses with little e-commerce experience.

Fortunately, the leaders at TalentTether quickly realized that to be successful, they would need to go to market in a new way.

"Over time we figured out the sales motions and skills that would be required to sell our new products. We invested in sales engineers so our sellers did not have to learn the nuances of every product. We also invested in sales development reps to handle prospecting and qualification of prospects, which made our sellers much more productive," shared one former executive.

The firm also quickly realized that investing in the online sales channel was not sufficient to win in the small- to medium-sized business market. They also had to rethink the customer success function and how they could support customer questions about career transition services before, during, and after delivery. "Even though we could deliver a lower touch sales experience upfront, we still needed a certain level of customer support throughout the process," said a former senior vice president of global marketing.

The firm invested more in marketing to generate more qualified leads, more finely segmented its customer universe, and ultimately executed a thorough rebrand in 2020, changing their name, brand promise, visuals, and go-to-market positioning to better reflect their "transformation into an end-to-end talent solutions provider with integrated digital offerings."

The changes paid off, and they had strong organic revenue growth for the first time in decades.

Overhauling their commercialization strategy made their productization efforts successful, and TalentTether avoided an unfortunate situation that we see repeatedly.

The situation goes like this. An organization decides to productize* and develops a differentiated new service, solution, or product that meets a *real* market need. BUT the new offering stalls after beta and does not generate the expected sales.

The product is a great idea, but the launch is a failure.

Why?

Because the organization underinvested in commercialization.

Through our experience guiding organizations to productize their services, we have found that most B2B services organizations who are productizing don't fully grasp the importance of developing a new and separate go-to-market strategy and adequately investing in different capabilities to execute a more productized go-to-market strategy.

We have a unique vantage point in that through the course of our work, we have hundreds of conversations with leaders at professional services firms each year about how they are transforming their busi-

---

* We define "productize" as the adaptation of a service that is delivered one-to-one or one-to-few into a product that can be delivered one-to-many. Product refers to a scalable, often tech-enabled, tool or program that can be packaged and sold to many customers. This could be as simple as just automating more of the work our professionals do with no change to how the client experiences the value delivery (productized services), to creating new products that clients use as a complement to our services (bundled solutions), to offering standalone products or products as a service to deliver value to new users and/or new market segments.

nesses through productization. We've looked across the spectrum of professions—legal, engineering, management consulting, IT services, Business Process Outsourcing (BPO), PR, marketing, and accounting—and we see this challenge over and over again:

Commercialization is the most significant stall point in productization.

One former chief revenue officer of a B2B services firm that unsuccessfully tried to productize described the problem well:

> *"There's this assumption that we'll just hand the new product over, and the sales team will sell it because 'It's new, it'll be exciting!'*

That's not the way it works.

> *There must be an end-to-end go-to-market strategy about who we are selling to, the pricing, the packaging, how we will generate leads, and what skills we need to sell, and **developing that strategy starts at the same time we begin developing the new product.**"*

We take some responsibility for this problem.

In our first book, *Productize: the Ultimate Guide to Turning Professional Services into Scalable Products*, we introduced the Productize Pathway®, a methodology specifically for B2B services organizations. It teaches organizations how to identify new product or solution opportunities, test the ideas quickly, develop new products with the help of customers, launch them, and then continue to manage them across their life cycle:

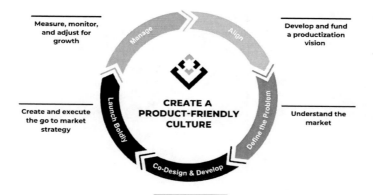

We devoted one chapter—Launch Boldly—to commercialization. As you can see in the circle, we also positioned the Launch Boldly phase as something that happens *after* the product is designed and developed.

In reality, you begin creating the building blocks of your commercialization strategy from the very beginning when you define the most attractive market segments and how your product will make money. You have a rough sense of how you will go to market before developing the concept. As you go along, you progressively add more validation and detail to your commercial models and business plans. The information that you collect to develop your productization vision and product design are inputs into your market segmentation, pricing and packaging, messaging, and sales channel decisions.

To fully understand this, let's start with defining "go-to-market."

What, Exactly, Is "Go-to-Market"?

The good news is that professional services firms already have a go-to-market strategy and capabilities. They are just designed to sell customized services. To successfully productize, you need a go-to-market strategy and capabilities that are designed for more scalable offerings.

Go-to-Market Strategy

A good go-to-market strategy answers the questions:

- What do we sell?
- To whom?
- How?

Unfortunately, a lot of organizations only think about one or two of these questions when they make the decision to develop a new product or solution.

Part of this is because the term "go-to-market" is not widely understood, especially in professional services. For example, one professional services leader who recently stepped into the role of go-to-market vice president shared with us:

> *"My primary challenge is that no one has a common definition for what go-to-market means. For example, some people think my role should be sales-focused such as defining the selling process, organizing the sales channel, and growing accounts. Other people think my role should focus on market strategy and marketing."*

Good go-to-market strategies and activities include **marketing, sales, *and* customer success**. And it starts with a strong understanding of customer needs and the competitive landscape.

The book *Product Launches* by Mary Sheehan defines "go-to market" as "a blueprint that details the strategy of how a company will target its existing customers and prospective customers with its value proposition and differentiation from the competition."[3]

We often see leaders confuse go-to-market strategy with hiring sales headcount. But it is so much more than that. Good go-to-market includes a whole ecosystem of activities including defining your market, creating your marketing strategy, determining how to generate leads, building sales collateral, sales compensation, and so on. In other words, a strong go-to-market strategy is NOT:

- A list of marketing campaigns
- A list of target customers
- Sales headcount

Go-to-Market Capabilities

When we talk about the ecosystem of go-to-market capabilities to successfully launch a new product, we are focused on five primary areas:

1. **Market Understanding**—Does the organization have a crisp description of who they are selling to and why? Do they understand customer needs by segments and understand the competitive environment? Does the organization have the processes and skills to continually discover new market insights to inform both product and go-to-market strategies?

2. **Pricing and Packaging**—Can the organization translate market understanding into a compelling business model that includes economically attractive product pricing and product packaging?

3. **Marketing**—Can the organization develop compelling messaging and communicate those messages using different marketing channels and generate the volume of leads necessary to meet revenue targets?

4. **Sales**—Does the organization have the sales channel and sales process to effectively sell the new product?

5. **Renewability**—Has the organization planned for account growth and product renewability?

The good news is that professional services organizations already have a go-to-market strategy—for customized services. When they decide to productize, they are required to operate at least two go-to-market models simultaneously—one that is robust and mature and one that is in start-up mode.

On top of that complexity, there is no one right go-to-market model for a productized service or pure product. The most effective go-to-market model will be determined by things such as the average contract value, number of deals, size of serviceable market, conversion rate, etc.

While we certainly see professional services firms develop products that do not meet customer needs fail, we also see products that do meet client needs fail because they do not have a sound go-to-market strategy or go-to-market capabilities.

The data supports this. In our most recent benchmarking survey of executives and product leaders in B2B professional services organizations, the second-highest-ranked productization challenge was "setting the right sales strategy, structure, and incentives," with 74 percent of respondents rating it difficult or very difficult.

We highly recommend assessing your own organization's commercialization readiness by taking a quick assessment at *https://www.vecteris.com/commercializationreadinessassessment*. This proprietary assessment will help you better understand you're the strengths and weaknesses of your organization's go-to-market capabilities for your productized offerings. Revisit the assessment as often as you like to track your progress and identify new areas of focus.

Here are a few indicators that a compelling product is hampered by a weak go-to-market strategy or capabilities:

1. *"We plan to sell the product using the same sales channel that has previously only sold customized services or solutions."*

2. *"We are going to sell the new product to a new market segment, but we do not have an engine to generate leads in this new market."*

3. *"My subscription product is not renewing."*

4. *"Multiple people are in charge of a new product's go-to-market strategy (e.g., head of product, CMO, head of sales)."*

5. *"The product pricing and packaging is putting our services revenue at risk of cannibalization."*

Professional services organizations that successfully commercialize more productized offerings do the following five things well:

1. Invest in new commercialization capabilities

2. Have clear owners for commercialization success

3. Begin building their commercialization strategy at the beginning of the product development cycle

4. Continue to iterate on their commercialization strategy after launch

5. Address cannibalization fears

Invest in New Commercialization Capabilities

Even in the early days when we are still validating our assumptions about the best go-to-market strategy for a new product, organizations need to make incremental, and new-to-organization, investments in marketing and sales. Those investments need to be accounted for when creating your case for productization or making a go/no-go decision on investing in a new product.

For example, if you are selling to a new market segment, you'll need an incremental marketing investment to reach the segment and generate leads. Even if you are selling to existing customers, you will need to do some product marketing, which you may not have the capability to do in-house if the only type of marketing you have historically done is brand building and maybe thought leadership when your consultants or partners have time to create it.

Or you may need a different sales channel. Or, at the very least, additional sales capacity. Selling products is different from selling services, so, depending on the type of solution you are launching, you may need to hire or develop new sales skills.

And don't forget about the cost to serve the new customers once acquired. For example, if it is a renewable product, that means ensuring customer satisfaction, so customers renew their subscriptions. Or, if the new product targets a new market segment, there may be additional costs to serving that market segment that must be considered.

Have Clear Owners for Commercialization Success

A tricky part about creating and executing successful commercialization strategies is that it requires *a lot* of cross-functional coordination. For example, as mentioned earlier, the sales function needs to be part of the initial product strategy discussions, as does marketing. In more mature organizations, there may be an executive in charge of "go-to-market," but for most organizations in early days of productization, one person does not own all the pieces. That means that silos and handoffs between services delivery, product, engineering, marketing, and sales need to be considered, as do the different incentives, reporting, and cultures of those functions. Building trust will be integral.

Start at the Beginning

Organizations should begin creating the building blocks of their product launch plan at the very beginning when they define the most attractive market segments and define how the product will make money. That means that sales and marketing executives also must be involved from the very beginning.

Unfortunately, at a lot of organizations, sales and marketing are left out of initial product strategy conversations. One chief revenue officer shared:

*"In my experience, there's a gross underestimation by the
product organization on how strategically helpful sales can
be in shaping product strategy early in. There isn't much
understanding or thought about how the existing sales
methodology, sales metrics, sales quotas, compensation, etc.
will affect a new product's success. Before our head of product
wants to launch something, I often say, 'This wasn't in our sales
plan for the year. Where is the funding for the additional sales
capacity that we will need?' Before building a product, you
need to align on how to sell and market the new product."*

When we begin to plan for the go-to-market early on, we can also
determine if we are prepared to make the investment needed to successfully bring the new product to market. As previously mentioned,
organizations are often not sufficiently investing in the go-to-market
capabilities needed to be successful.

Continue to Iterate after Launch

Successfully commercializing does not mean launching with certainty.
It means launching with a set of assumptions that you quickly test.
Your assumptions will be informed by earlier tests and will, hopefully,
be directionally correct, but it is a big mistake to assume that your
pricing, packaging, messaging, ideal customer profile, marketing tactics, and sales approach will not evolve over time.

It takes a while to achieve what is called "go-to-market fit*," and
the only way to do this is to experiment in real market conditions. This
can be incredibly uncomfortable for leaders of companies who are new
to innovation and are not used to experimenting and learning from

---

* Go-to-market fit refers to having an effective and scalable strategy for selling and
delivering your product to customers beyond just having a product that meets market
needs (product-market fit). You typically do not achieve this until you achieve $3–$5
million in revenue.

both successes and failures. Learning through intelligent experimentation is not a well-developed muscle at most B2B services companies, as we discussed at length in our book *Fearless: How to Transform a Services Culture and Successfully Productize*.

For example, since the winter of 2022, many professional services firms have been experimenting with how to use generative AI to improve the efficiency of their work. As they achieve more efficiencies in billable work, they must rethink their pricing models. For example, as the number of hours to conduct an audit decline because of automation through AI, some accounting firms are switching from time-and-materials pricing to fixed-fee pricing or a hybrid of fixed-fee and time and materials. As AI continues to improve, many firms are raising their hourly billing rates to account for the cost of the new technology or they're switching entirely to fixed-fee pricing. To experiment well, they need to develop hypotheses about how different pricing models and price points will impact demand and profitability and then test these hypotheses through experimentation.

Iteration through experimentation is a capability that is only going to increase in importance. The pace of change is coming faster, which requires nimble thinking and behavior. The most important thing to remember is that **your go-to-market strategy and launch plan do not need to be perfect before starting**. You only need to be transparent about the outcomes you are expecting from the go-to-market decisions you have made, and the strategy needs to include a plan to iterate as you learn if your decisions and tactics yield the expected outcomes.

Additionally, as you learn more about how to successfully commercialize your product and change direction or tactics, you must consider the knock-on effects of your decisions. For example, if you change the ideal client profile for a product, you likely need to change marketing tactics, competitive differentiation, and maybe even the sales channel.

Why You Need New Commercialization Capabilities

If you want to successfully productize, you will likely be required to operate at least two go-to-market models simultaneously—one that is appropriate for customized services and one that is designed for more scalable offerings.

Marketing and selling a more productized solution are very different from marketing and selling a customized service. For starters, when you are selling a customized service, you are focused on understanding customer needs and then convincing a customer that your organization has the capabilities to meet those needs. Customers are buying the promise that the people will be able to meet their needs. Or, as one managing partner described it, *"Our clients are buying 'Yes-as-a-Service.'"*

But a service that has been productized has to be positioned as the best packaging of features for a set price to meet the common need of a customer segment.

In other words, services are bought, and products are sold. Greg Alexander, founder of sales consulting firm SBI, described it like this:

> *"If I'm a customer and I'm considering buying a product, I'm buying the features of the product, the tangible benefit of the product . . . And I might never even talk to a salesperson. And even if I do talk to a salesperson, it's not part of my evaluation criteria. What's part of my evaluation criteria is the quality of the product. I can separate people from the product.*
>
> *Services, on other hand, are just the opposite. I can't separate the person from the service because the person* is *the service."*[4]

It is important to acknowledge that many B2B services organizations that are introducing products or productized services are doing so alongside existing services or as part of a bundled solution that includes both services and more productized services/products. That means that **this is not as simple as standing up a products go-to-market orga-**

nization. Launching products alongside solutions is more complex and requires an approach that is different from pure services commercialization and products commercialization (more on that later).

Product Marketing Is Different from Services Marketing

Good product marketing is typically focused on customer niches, articulating their problems, and describing how a product solves those problems. It is very different from the broader brand building and thought-leadership marketing that a services firm may do to promote their expertise or build brand awareness.

For example, we worked with one accounting and consulting firm, who, after successful alpha and beta pilots, was launching a new bundled solution that included consulting services plus data and software in select markets. Creating the go-to-market strategy and toolkit was a collaborative effort between the product team, the consulting team, and the global marketing team. It quickly became obvious, however, that the marketing team was woefully under-resourced to support a product launch. They had the budget and expertise to identify conferences to sponsor and whitepapers to write, but they did not have expertise at creating product demo videos or generating new-to-firm leads with a customer-problem-first approach.

Another big factor that could dramatically change the marketing resources needed is whether the product or productized service will be sold to existing customers or new customers. If new customers are the target, lead generation resources will be needed and at a scale higher than you may have used to bring in new services clients because, as evidenced in benchmarks, conversion rates and contract value is typically lower. That means you'll need more leads if you want your product revenue to match or surpass your services revenue.

Additionally, you may be targeting new market segments that you have less familiarity with reaching and little brand recognition with. For example, an accounting firm we worked with developed compliance workflow software that could be applied to emerging healthcare regulations. They needed to learn how to sell to chief medical officers at midsized hospital systems (their ideal customer profile) to successfully commercialize the opportunity. This was a completely different buyer than their traditional accounting services buyer.

New and Different Sales Channels

Successfully selling products, productized services, or even bundled solutions requires a different sales muscle than most services organizations have. A very common mistake is expecting that your existing sellers—whether you have doer-sellers or a dedicated sales force—will be able to sell a more productized offering.

For example, many professional services firms—especially law firms, accounting firms, and even consulting firms—have doer-sellers. A doer-seller (or seller-doer) is a billable professional who balances delivering client project work with taking purposeful actions to help generate new business and revenue for their firm. They typically spend 10–30 percent of their time on business development, which means that their sales skills are typically less mature. Their experience is in selling themselves and/or customized services rather than selling products.

Other firms have dedicated sellers who focus on bringing in new clients. But assuming service sellers can effectively sell products is also a mistake.

Selling products requires different skills and a different process. For example, product sellers are effective at value-based selling versus the cost-plus model* that many professional services firms use. Good product sellers demonstrate product value in the sales process. They have experience using product demos, for example, as part of the sales process. In contrast, a product demo for a services sale is usually thought

---

* This refers to the practice of pricing services or products based on the cost to deliver or create it, such as determining the price by adding a fixed percentage or "markup" to the cost to create or deliver.

leadership pieces that are given away to demonstrate firm expertise, and the doer-seller or delivery lead provides free advice to the prospect in the sales process to demonstrate the future client experience.

In the product-sales process, if the product is tech-enabled, a technical buyer like a chief information officer may be involved, which means that the seller needs experience working with technical buyers. There is less customization and deal flexibility, and because of the lower contract value we showed earlier, there is also often higher volume.

Andrea Fryear, CEO of Agile Sherpas, an Agile methods-training company, learned this lesson the hard way when they introduced an online learning platform. She shared,

> *"When we started including an online learning platform with training deals, the buyers immediately brought IT into the sales process. And then we were in this huge, complicated IT procurement world. They started treating us like a technology vendor instead of a training provider, asking for all this complicated compliance stuff, and before you know it, the SOW is taking six months longer to get approved."*

The seniority of the buyer may also vary from your traditional services buyer. For example, the buyer may also end up being more junior, especially if the productized service or offering is at a lower price point. For example, one consulting company that we work with sold their traditional working capital analysis services to the CEO or CFO. They expanded their offerings by developing a software solution for companies who had their own internal cost analysis teams. The firm's chief product officer shared, "The C-level buyers want advisory services and insights, but their teams just want our products. Our traditional sellers over-index on selling advice to CFOs rather than selling our products to their teams."

Even if you are selling your products as part of a bundle that includes traditional services, it is unlikely that your traditional sellers will be successful without some additional support. For example, the head of one HR advisory firm estimates that there was a "cap" on how much product revenue a traditional services seller could sell. He said, *"They were so used to selling expertise that they could only cover about 20 to 30 percent of our product sales goal. We had to hit the rest with a dedicated product sales force."*

Renewability

The last significant difference between services go-to-market motions and product go-to-market motions is that many products are sold on a renewable subscription basis. This difference is especially significant for services businesses that sell projects rather than retainers. For project-based businesses, it is a big leap to build the capabilities that ensure their customers have a multiyear journey using the product.

The biggest underlying component of renewability is that renewable revenue requires recurring impact. For example, we worked with a training organization that created an online subscription-based training product, but the bulk of the impact customers received was through two training interventions that happened relatively early in the life of the subscription. Only 30 percent of customers continued beyond a year.

You'll also need robust systems for managing ongoing customer relationships. This involves tracking customer interactions, preferences, and feedback to ensure satisfaction and retention. It includes investing in analytics to understand customer usage patterns, preferences, and churn risks.

The most common function you'll need to add is customer success. Customer success is a support system focused on helping subscribers get the most out of their subscriptions, including onboarding, troubleshooting, and regular check-ins. A dedicated customer success team can proactively work to increase customer satisfaction, reduce churn, and drive upsells or cross-sells.

Why Read *Commercialize*?

Many books and resources cover the key steps in productization such as digital transformation, innovation, product management, and business model transformation. There is also research about switching from on-premises products to SaaS-style products-as-a-service, and an overwhelming amount of general sales strategy best practices.

But there's almost nothing on how to *transform* your go-to-market strategy to either sell more productized services or how to introduce products alongside services. **The very little that does exist on how to develop and scale go-to-market capabilities is written for brand-new products and tech-native businesses.**

Commercialization Expertise Is Thin

There are many resources on how to effectively sell products. They typically focus on a generalized sales framework such as MEDDIC*, Challenger†, or Value Selling‡.

There are also many resources for how to innovate, design, and develop great products. Their primary focus tends to be on building a user-centric product that can scale or Agile coaches who train in-house development teams on how to develop products with higher velocity, flexibility, and user-focus.

---

* Metrics, Economic Buyer, Decision Criteria, Decision Process, Identify Pain, and Champion (MEDDIC), is a sales methodology that focuses on qualifying leads thoroughly. It's particularly useful in complex B2B sales environments, helping sales teams understand the buying process and key drivers behind a potential purchase.

† Based on the idea that salespeople should challenge customers' thinking, this approach encourages sales teams to teach, tailor, and take control of sales interactions. It emphasizes delivering insights that reframe how customers think about their problems and solutions.

‡ This methodology centers on communicating the value that the customer will receive from the product or service, beyond just its features or technical specifications. It involves quantifying the benefits in terms of ROI, efficiency gains, cost savings, or other metrics important to the customer.

But there are very few resources that answer critical commercialization questions such as:

- How do I know if our product concept is ready for commercialization?
- How long will it take to successfully commercialize a new product?
- What different marketing tactics should I use to generate leads for my product?
- What sales channels are best for my product?
- How do I build a sales process for my product?
- If my product is renewable, how do I design the product for recurring impact?
- If my product is renewable, what types of investments do I need to make in customer success?
- What is the best go-to-market strategy if my products are bundled with existing services?

Sales Training & Development	Gap: Commercializing New Products	Product Development
• Tech/product sales training (e.g., Force Management) assumes tech baseline - too high level maturity for services organizations	• How do I know if our product concept is ready to commercialize?	• Many application developers who will run high-level design sprints and develop MVPs +
• Focuses on the what (methodology) and now the how (making the switch from services to product)	• How long will it take to commercialize a new product?	• Focus on building a product that can sell (vs a product that has real market-demand or is likely to renew)
• Generalized sales frameworks (e.g., MEDDICC)	• Should I create a separate sales and GTM team for my product(s)?	• Many 'agile coach' providers who teach in-house development teams how to develop with higher velocity and flexibility
	• How do I build a sales process for products / bundled products for services?	

Commercializing Products in a Services Organization Is Very Different from Commercializing Products in a Products Organization

The few resources on how to successfully commercialize new innovations and launch new products are all written for business leaders at product-native companies such as software-as-a-service start-ups. Some of our favorites include *The Go-to-Market Handbook for B2B SaaS Leaders* by Richard Blundell or Ulrik Lehrskov-Schmidt's *The Pricing Roadmap: How to Design B2B SaaS Pricing Models That Your Customers Will Love,* but their frameworks can be difficult for B2B services organizations to adopt thanks to the nuances involved when pricing products that are sold alongside or bundled with services.

These resources are insufficient if you are launching products/productized services in a company that is purpose-built to market and sell *services.* For example, unless you are creating a standalone products business with money from outside investors, you cannot use sales performance benchmarks from product-native companies that are often funded by venture capital. Keep in mind your unique strategy and balance sheet structure when setting performance targets.

One of the key differences between selling products when you are a products firm and selling products when you are a services firm is that often you may be bundling your products into existing services, selling them to complement services, or trying to sell products in a way that do not cannibalize your existing revenue streams.

Often Sold with Services

In *Productize*, we introduced a simple framework to help organizations visualize the different ways they may productize their services.

Productization Ladder for Services Organizations

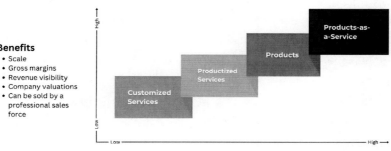

Benefits
- Scale
- Gross margins
- Revenue visibility
- Company valuations
- Can be sold by a professional sales force

Use of Technology

To grasp the opportunity for bundling, it's helpful to understand the four different types of productization available to services organizations:

1. Customized services are human-resource intensive and delivered differently for each client.

2. Productized services still require people to deliver, but fewer people are needed than for customized services because the service delivery is standardized, often in predefined packages that can be configured.

3. Products are off-the-shelf solutions purchased at one point in time, such as a course, toolkit, or data set.

4. Products-as-a-service take a product offering and keep the service ongoing for a subscription fee. Models include software-as-a-service, data-as-a-service, and learning-as-a-service.

As we move from customized services in the lower left to products-as-a-service in the upper right, the use of technology tends to increase (the x-axis), as do the benefits (the y-axis). Benefits include improved gross margins, better revenue visibility, and increased company valuation.

Many B2B services organizations who productize start by bundling products in with existing services. For example, the law firm Vorys developed eControl, which includes a platform for brands to monitor and manage authorized sellers across distribution channels along with legal services that help brands create authorized seller policies and compliance standards.

Or the products may not be bundled with services but may complement services and be sold to existing services customers. For example, Mercer, a global leader in HR consulting and employee health and benefits, provides comprehensive solutions such as Skills-Edge Suite, Employee Rewards, and Employee Experience Insights, which combine data, technology, and advisory services to deliver value. The mix of products and services is customized based on the maturity level of the client.

When done well, this complementary approach can act like rocket fuel for the business and provide a significant competitive advantage. This is because complementary products can be bundled with services in attractive packages that offer better value or convenience to the customer than standalone offerings. Bundling can also encourage the trial use of new products and increase the stickiness of your offerings. Introducing complementary products opens cross-selling opportunities, allowing you to leverage existing relationships and sales channels to promote new offerings. This strategy can lead to a more diversified revenue stream, reducing reliance on a single product or service line.

This services + products bundled solution approach brings a whole host of questions that are not well addressed in existing literature. For example:

- How do you encourage existing services sellers to bundle products with services or cross-sell products to existing customers?

- If developing a product sales channel, who owns customer relationships, services sellers or product sellers?

- If the solution crosses practice areas, what is the best way to effectively coordinate?

- How do you mitigate the risk of the products cannibalizing services revenue (or vice versa)?

- How do you ensure that products are not "given away for free" or overly discounted to services customers (assuming the products are not a loss leader strategy)?

- How do you position the product to existing services buyers?

- When bundling products with services, how do you still make it easy for customers to understand what they are buying? How do you avoid confusing the market with too much complexity?

Heather Ryan, partner and global product leader at Mercer, oversees Mercer's Skills Edge Solution, which is a bundle of advisory services, data, and technology. Although the solution has been a resounding success, positioning Mercer as a leader supporting companies' transformation to thinking about compensation based on skills not jobs, its launch had challenges. Heather shared a few that they faced:

> *"Bundling services with products into one solution can bring forward questions and complexity when working with clients. An offering needs to be simple enough for people (internally and externally) to understand the value and power of the*

combination. When we offered our Skills Edge Solution, we worked to create a crisp message of the power of consulting with products. It did take several iterations with our marketing team to get the messaging to emphasize that the solution was consulting, data, and tech—the power was in the combination, not the parts."

"Another challenge is that service teams may fear they are hitting the upper bounds of a client's project appetite when a big project requires a combination of data, services, and tech. Additionally, tech inclusion might require another set of approvers on the client side (like a data security or IT team member) and hence broadens the work to sign a contract. Crafting an offering of services, data, and tech requires making the value of the combination very clear AND making it easy to sign a client up for all the parts."

The instinct to protect services revenue at the expense of product revenue is another unique challenge that B2B services organizations face when they launch new products.

Fear of Cannibalization May Shut Off Certain Commercialization Strategies

Another reason why services firms introducing new products cannot just follow a "launch new products" playbook is because the fear of cannibalization.

For example, Prevedere, an economic forecasting company we work with, started as a services provider, building forecast models and maintaining those models for its clients. It has since developed a software and data product designed for the data scientists directly employed by their clients to build and maintain their own models. But they historically have been reluctant to unbundle the product and sell it without the services because it may cannibalize higher-priced enterprise deals that include services revenue. Rich Wagner, the chief executive officer described the dilemma like this:

> *"We recently did a multi-million-dollar deal with one of our customers where 75% of the revenue is from the software license and 25% is from the upfront forecasting model set-up services fee. But many traditional software companies sell individual software licenses to try software before advancing to enterprise deals. There may be an opportunity for Prevedere to offer the software license in a similar way, and we will need to ensure customers can self-serve and get value as fast."*

Ignoring market segments that will buy products only is something that less mature professional services organizations will do. It makes sense because of all the benefits of selling products alongside or bundled with services discussed earlier.

If, however, you want to fully sunset services and become a product business, you should start from scratch and leverage the wealth of product pure play resources that already exist. Which is why it is so important to tailor your go-to-market approach based on your productization strategy and the maturity of your offerings.

Strategy and Maturity Matters

The sequence in which you build different go-to-market capabilities will depend on your productization strategy, as well as the maturity of the product or solution.

For example, you don't want to invest in long-term marketing plans and sales capabilities before truly validating product market fit and growth tactics. Investing in a dedicated salesforce for a product that does not have established product-market fit is premature. As you validate product-market fit and your go-to-market strategy, making more investments in maturing marketing, revenue operations, sales, and customer success is appropriate. Expectations need to be set clearly with the leadership team that this will be a test-and-learn process. As you test and learn more, you will invest more, but there should not be multiyear marketing plans for a brand-new product launch. That would be a waste of time and resources.

Similarly, if you are launching a product that will be sold to a new market segment like a more price-sensitive segment, your go-to-market strategy and capability needs will be *completely* different than if you are selling a solution that bundles products with services being sold to your current target markets.

Productization Strategy Matters

There are four general strategies for professional services organizations that are productizing:

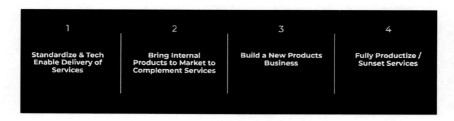

Some organizations pursue multiple strategies if they have the capabilities and sufficient market demand. Some organizations may transition through different strategies as their capabilities mature and the market evolves.

The go-to-market motions—(1) **Market Understanding**, (2) **Pricing and Packaging**, (3) **Marketing**, (4) **Sales,** and (5) **Renewability**—apply to all four strategies, but how they are implemented varies. As we'll discuss later, the correct go-to-market model for a product will be dependent on several variables such as the average contract value, size of serviceable market, and your sales conversion rate.

For example, if you decide to sell standalone products rather than just use products to enable solutions delivery, each product will need its own go-to-market and customer success capabilities. If you decide to sell products to existing customers, existing services staff will need to support the strategy and be involved in the product creation process.

#1—Standardize and Tech-Enable Delivery of Services

This strategy focuses on codifying and standardizing how services are delivered, often using technology to automate parts of the process. Clients may be unaware that the products are being used. For example, Euromonitor International, a data analytics and consulting firm, standardized and tech-enabled eight core consulting offerings. By focusing on just a handful of standard offerings, they reduced customization, reduced overhead management of sales and delivery, and provided customers a higher quality and consistent experience. At first glance, you may not think that this product needs a go-to-market strategy and capabilities. But this strategy still requires (1) understanding the needs of the internal users; (2) an estimate of the value generated by the product, such as efficiency gains, that will result from use of the product to guide product investment decisions; (3) internal marketing to persuade internal staff to use the new product; and (4) customer success to ensure that the product is used well and continually.

#2—Bring Products to Market to Complement Services

This strategy takes the processes and tools that standardize the delivery of services, turns them into products, and sells them externally alongside services. These products augment services offered, sustain services delivered, or reduce the cost of services delivered.

For example, STEP, a managed IT services in the connectivity space, launched a software offering that helps its customers derive real-time, global visibility into 5G site reliability. Originally developed as a platform for STEP's consultants to use, STEP began bundling it as a solution with its service offerings, shifting to a train-the-trainer enablement model.

When it comes to launching products that coexist with core offerings, the go-to-market strategy becomes more complex in areas like pricing, where the side effects on services revenue need to be considered, or like sales channel decisions where you want to leverage existing relationships but also have services sellers who are not used to selling products. In other areas, like marketing, the strategy may be simpler because you are marketing to an existing market segment where you already have brand awareness and existing relationships with buyers.

#3—Build a New Products Business

When organizations face a fundamental disruption or find highly attractive adjacencies, they often launch new product businesses. This strategy can be a good way to learn while starting new revenue streams that have the potential to overtake the services business over time.

For example, AMEND, a consulting firm that works with mid-market Midwestern growth-minded industrial companies, created Batched, a SaaS-based dynamic production-scheduling tool for the printing industry. After the product's successful alpha and beta phases, AMEND created a separate business for the product and is actively scaling the business separately from its core consulting business. They also found a channel partner, an existing provider of software, for the label printing and flexible packaging segments that allowed them to directly sell to an already warm list of companies. For organizations following this strategy, pricing and sales channel decisions may be simpler, but more investment may be required because the go-to-market capabilities may be separate and dedicated.

#4—Productize the Core

For organizations facing significant competition or looking for a sharp increase in growth, creating a pure productized business is a go-big strategy. This is a complete business model transformation and requires a much more significant transformation in go-to-market tactics, roles, and talent. If this is your productization strategy, you are best served by building a new go-to-market organization almost from scratch. Some organizations may choose to maintain services to customize product implementation only, while others will fully sunset their services business.

Maturity Matters

If you have just launched a new offering making less than $1 million in product revenue, your approach to finding customers will be different than if you are making $100 million-plus a year in product revenue.

When you first launch, you need to have a set of *hypotheses* or a vision of how you will attract and sell to customers, so you can start to test those hypotheses early. You'll need a plan for how to test your more mature go-to-market strategies early and the flexibility to learn and refine them.

In other words, how do you successfully launch new productized offerings so you don't set yourself up for failure later?

Early on, you'll need to validate the assumptions in your initial launch plan.

- Do you have the right ideal customer profile (ICP)?

- Is your pricing appropriate? Your packaging?

- Is the customer buyer journey really what you initially mapped out?

- What are the best ways to generate leads?

- How effective are the different sales channels?

- Is the product truly renewable?

- What investments do you need to make to improve sales effectiveness? Renewability?

As you validate hypotheses, you invest more. **You do not create a mature sales team or have a year-long marketing plan on day one.**

In our experience, there is a right amount of investment at each level of maturity. The sequence in which you invest more will depend on the productization strategy considerations discussed earlier. For example, you will invest more in lead generation as you learn more about how to attract customers, but if you are selling to existing customers, your lead-generation investment will always be less than if you're selling to a new market segment.

We've identified four stages of launch and go-to-market evolution for B2B services companies who are launching new productized offerings. These "rules of thumb" can vary widely depending on the type of offering, market conditions, and specific organization risk appetite and balance sheet strength. However, there are general guidelines and litmus tests that can be applied at each stage.

These have some overlap with the different funding stages that a venture capitalist may consider when investing in a start-up with some important caveats for organizations that are NOT start-ups, are likely self-funding the new offering from existing cash flow, have to keep the rest of the business growing, and may be measuring the success of beyond revenue to include its impact on other parts of the business (efficiency, share of wallet, etc.).

Stage 0—Discovery and Testing

This includes the up-front market research and testing a minimum viable product (MVP)* with a handful of customers (typically called alpha). The goal of this stage is to decide whether to pursue developing the product beyond its MVP.

It's never too early to start go-to-market activities, and they must be an integral part of the discovery and testing process. Before you build anything, it is important to build up-front market research capabilities that are ideally continuous and that deliver customer insights to the prioritization process and early demand testing. At this stage, you are focused on understanding customer needs, the competitive landscape, and creating hypotheses about the buyer journey and the likely go-to-market strategy and resources needed in future stages.

If you have a marketing function with strong market research skills, they may help with this stage, or you may have a dedicated experienced product manager run this independently, or you may outsource to an experienced consulting firm or contractor. You will create initial messaging and personas and basic tools to attract alpha customers, such as a one-sheet or a simple pitch deck. The go-to-market strategy is often experimental, involving a lot of customer feedback and iteration.

There is no revenue at this stage, and the only benefits may be increasing the loyalty of the alpha customers and identifying one-off services opportunities.

The exception here is if you are following a funding model where you have one or several customers funding the product development as part of a services engagement. For example, sometimes a services client will ask for a custom technology solution as part of engagement, and

---

* The MVP concept comes from *The Lean Startup* by Eric Ries, which posits that traditional, linear waterfall development or R&D stage gates should be replaced by iterative, agile techniques. Ries defines it as "the smallest experiment that either proves or disproves [our] assumptions about a business idea."

you negotiate a deal to own the intellectual property so you can more broadly productize the tool. In this case, you may have revenue from the offering, but you will still need to validate if customers outside of the initial alpha customers have a need for the offering and are willing to pay for it.

Stage 1—Validating Product-Market Fit

This includes an initial pilot to a market segment subset to refine messaging, pricing, and demand generation tactics (sometimes called a closed beta).

The goal of this stage is to determine if you have product-market fit, which means businesses in an attractive market segment want and are willing to pay for your product. You are testing the value proposition, validating that you have the best target segment, and learning how to reach the target market most efficiently and effectively[5].

This can start in what is traditionally called the "concept testing and design" phase where you're talking to clients or prospective clients and collecting feedback on the concept idea prior to development. Here, you're also honing your sales pitch. Ideally, you're also asking the million-dollar question at the end of the concept testing interview: *"Do you want to be a beta customer?"*

In this stage, sales and marketing is the job of the product leader. The product lead is still acting like a mini general manager or "founder" for the business opportunity represented by the product. Think of the product leader at this stage as a brand manager owning the validation of their earlier decisions on "where to play" (strategy), "what to build" (product design), and "how to win" (go-to-market). They must not only be great at listening to the market but also at translating that into a profitable business model, which includes the product cost structure and go-to-market capabilities. This is *not* an easy skill set to find, so think carefully about who will play this role[6].

Whitney Gibson, chair and founder of the law firm Vorys's eControl practice shared:

> *"Who you get to lead this is the most important decision that you'll make. For us, someone who has led a product in a service-heavy industry but also had data-platform experience was ideal. The person we have has very strong commercial and business acumen and was able to come in and adjust product costs but also make sure that as software development costs decrease, we increase sales and marketing costs. He's also willing to do whatever it takes for us to hit our targets."*

We also suggest investing in a junior customer success resource at this stage if there isn't one in the organization and having that function temporarily report to the product leader.

You may allow a small part of your existing sales team to begin to sell the product and enlist your existing marketing team's support in generating initial leads, but most of the go-to-market activities will be led by the product leader. This resourcing keeps the product lead focused on refining the value proposition and the go-to-market strategy for a broader launch.

Our benchmarking data supports this. In the early phases of productization maturity, *100 percent* of organizations do not put in place dedicated sales for products[7]. You don't want to invest in additional sales or marketing support until you know that you have product-market fit. There is minimal budget spent on demand generation, with a focus on cost-effective channels like outreach to existing or previous customers, organic social (LinkedIn), organic search and content marketing (including webinars), product websites, and initial demo videos. You will also begin to collect testimonials to support the next phase.

If your product success is being measured primarily by recurring revenue, you'll stay in this stage until you get to about $1 million in annual recurring revenue (ARR) or ten to twenty paying customers with some important exceptions if the business case for the offering included increasing efficiency of delivery of other services or selling other services, in which case you'll need targets for those other success measures to help you decide if you have product-market fit or not.

Stage 2—Validating Go-to-Market Fit

In this stage, you are validating that you have go-to-market fit, which is when you know how to attract the interest of the market segments that you are targeting (i.e., marketing) and you know how to convert them into paid customers (i.e., sales). Go-to-market fit includes knowing how to price and package the product and means that you have consistency in sales/buying process, delivery, and outcomes[8].

Our benchmarking data shows that organizations at this stage are much more likely to put in place dedicated product sales and dedicated customer success or account management teams. They recognize the value of professionals who know how to sell and renew products. At this stage, roughly 25 percent of organizations utilize a separate sales team for product, over 45 percent utilize a single sales team, and less than 20 percent rely on doer-sellers[9].

In this stage, you will create your sales playbook (sales method, what you say, tools you use, etc.) before hiring a dedicated sales force or investing in training the broader existing sales channels. As you validate go-to-market fit, you make investments in dedicated sales and product marketing and maybe also in growth marketing to quickly try and validate new demand and lead generation tactics.

If your product success is being measured primarily by recurring revenue, you'll stay in this stage until you get to about $3 million–$5 million in ARR and have validated that you have figured out how to generate a strong flow of leads in your target market(s).

At this stage, you also invest in more dedicated customer success and/or account management to ensure that new customers are onboarded effectively and that customers use and renew the offering (if applicable).

If you are selling a solution that bundles services with more scalable content, tech, and/or data products, this is the stage where you want to start decreasing the amount of the solution's value that comes from the less scalable customized services and increase the amount that comes from the more scalable components. When this happens, you can reduce your reliance on doer-sellers and start to expect more of the solutions revenue to come from a salesforce experienced in product sales.

Stage 3—Scale-Up

At this stage, you have a clear vision of how to grow the product business into a $10 million-plus business and begin investing substantially more resources into marketing, such as a dedicated product marketer to manage marketing new features as well as larger scale investments in paid ads, PR, conference sponsorship, and higher-end videos. You'll make more investments in sales, such as inside sales, as well as begin to expand into new geographic markets or target other market segments.

At this point, you may also redeploy your launch product leader to focus on new products and bring in a more technical product leader.

The conventional wisdom is that you want to get to this stage within eighteen to thirty-six months of validating product-market fit, but if you have a tech-centric product such as a piece of software or AI-powered solution, the market is likely evolving so quickly that you'll want to reach this stage within nine to eighteen months of validating product-market fit[10].

In this stage, you are focused on increasing pricing, increasing your conversion rates, and decreasing the sales cycle.

If you are selling a solution that bundles services with more scalable content, tech, and/or data products, this is the stage where you also start selling just the product—without the services—to new market segments who either do not need the services because of their own in-house capabilities or who are more price sensitive and do not want to pay for customization. At this stage, it is important to manage cannibalization fear, so that you can continue to grow, and manage cannibalization risk so you don't inadvertently erode services revenue.

We'll revisit the appropriate tactics for each maturity stage in the subsequent chapters, but here is a sneak peek of what we'll cover:

Stage	Outcome	Key Activities	Revenue	Team/ Resources	Go-to-Market Approach
0: Discovery and Testing	Decision on whether to pursue product development beyond MVP	• Market research • MVP testing with alpha customers • Initial messaging and persona creation • Basic marketing tools development	None (typically)	Marketing function or dedicated product manager Possible outsourcing to consultants	Experimental, with heavy customer feedback and iteration
1: Validating Product-Market Fit	Determine if product-market fit exists	• Pilot to market segment subset • Refine messaging, pricing, and demand generation tactics • Concept testing and design • Beta customer recruitment	Minimal (aiming for $1M ARR or 10-20 paying customers depending on product type)	Product leader as "mini general manager" Junior customer success resource Limited existing sales and marketing support	Product leader-driven, with a focus on cost-effective channels (e.g., existing customers, organic social, content marketing)
2: Validating Go-to-Market Fit	Confirm ability to attract and convert target market segments	-Create sales playbook -Invest in dedicated sales and product marketing -Validate lead generation tactics -Improve customer onboarding and retention	$3M-$5M ARR	Dedicated product sales team (in ~25% of organizations) Dedicated customer success/ account management Growth marketing	Increased investment in sales and marketing, with focus on repeatable processes
3: Scale-Up	Grow product business to $10M+	• Substantial marketing investments (paid ads, PR, conferences) • Expand to new geographic markets or segments • Focus on increasing pricing, conversion rates, and decreasing sales cycle • Possible unbundling of product from services	$10M+	Dedicated product marketer Expanded sales team (e.g., inside sales) Possible transition to more technical product leader	Large-scale, multi-channel approach with significant resource allocation

If Successfully Productizing Is So Hard, Why Do It?

Many strong pressures and opportunities make productization an attractive strategy for growth. In *Productize*, we outlined the business case for productizing, which included improving margins, increasing valuation, and fending off digital-first competitors. Since publishing *Productize*, the business case for productizing has been further strengthened as advancements in AI threaten to disrupt professional services firms. This business case includes:

- Companies that have productized are more profitable, grow faster, and achieve higher valuations compared to their peers.

- The market is changing. Most companies are quickly becoming digital businesses and generative AI is both a threat and an incredible opportunity for services businesses.

- B2B buyer behavior has evolved. B2B buyers now prefer subscription-based products since they are easier to budget for and grow in value. Buyers prefer on-demand purchasing and want alternative options for faster, lower-touch ways to engage with sellers.

- The customized services model strains and stresses your talent. Not only are custom services projects more difficult on delivery teams, but they require more specialized talent.

Key Takeaways

1. Most B2B services organizations that are productizing don't fully grasp the importance of developing a new and separate go-to-market strategy and adequately investing in different capabilities to execute a more productized go-to-market strategy.

2. While we certainly see professional services firms develop products that do not meet customer needs fail, we also see products that *do* meet client needs fail because they are not commercialized well.

3. You create the building blocks of your commercialization plan from the very beginning of designing your productization strategy when you identify the most attractive market segments and define how your product will make money. You fine-tune your commercialization strategy throughout the entire product development cycle.

4. Professional services organizations already have a go-to-market strategy—for customized services. When they decide to productize, they are required to operate at least two go-to-market models simultaneously—one that is designed to sell services and is robust and mature and one that is designed to sell a more productized offering and is in start-up mode.

5. Good go-to-market plans and activities include marketing, sales, and customer success.

6. There is no one right go-to-market model for a productized service or pure product. The correct model will be dependent on things such as your productization strategy, the offering's maturity as well as variables such as the average contract value, the size of serviceable market, and conversion rate.

7. Existing resources on how to successfully commercialize new innovations and launch new products are insufficient if you are launching products/productized services in a company that is purpose-built to market and sell services.

8. One of the key differences between selling products when you are a products firm and selling products when you are a services firm is that often you may be bundling your products

into existing services, selling them to complement services or, at least, trying to sell products in a way that do not cannibalize your existing revenue streams.

Additional Resources

We highly recommend assessing your own organization's commercialization readiness by taking a quick assessment at *https://www.vecteris. com/commercializationreadinessassessment.* This proprietary assessment will help you better understand you're the strengths and weaknesses of your organization's go-to-market capabilities for your productized offerings. Revisit the assessment as often as you like to track your progress and identify new areas of focus.

Furthermore, throughout the book, we've included references to *Commercialize* tools that help with the implementation of tactics and strategies for developing the go-to-market strategy for new services and products. For example, sample sales playbooks, job descriptions, customer persona grids, and much more are located online. Just look for this icon ✗ and go to *www.commercializebook.com* to download the tools.

CHAPTER 2

DECIDING WHO TO SELL TO (A.K.A. MARKET UNDERSTANDING)

Why We Start with Who

Choosing the right market(s) and understanding the needs of the market is where all great commercialization strategy starts. This includes:

- Which customers will be interested in this new product?

- Who is the buyer at those customer organizations?

- What are the characteristics or personas of each target customer segment?

- What problems will this new product solve for each segment?

- How will they view this product versus competitive alternatives?

- What are the most attractive market segments to pursue?

Deciding WHO the best target market is for your new solution is the most important go-to-market decision you'll make because it influences everything else. Decisions about pricing, packaging, positioning, marketing channels, and sales channels all start with your target market.

For example, TalentTether* realized that the firm was spending a lot of money to land agreements with small to midmarket companies to provide customized outplacement services but was seeing little growth following customer acquisition. This is because midmarket companies typically had less frequent needs (e.g., more episodic layoffs) and smaller budgets than larger companies. One former executive described the strategy as: "We wanted to repurpose the time of our talented team members from relationship management of accounts that had limited potential to grow their spending with us to expanding the wallet share and product portfolio diversity within larger accounts. It was a big opportunity to improve customer profitability."

The firm made a smart business decision and created a more productized offering for the smallest companies with infrequent outplacement needs and limited budgets. But this decision to create a more standardized, lower-priced product for a different market segment had *significant* go-to-market consequences.

For example, a former head of global marketing shared,

> *"We were a sales organization that was built for long sales cycles and large contract values. Initially, we thought the existing sales team would sell the new product, but we quickly found out that the sales motion was different—it was more transactional, quicker, and the value proposition was different. It also required a different marketing strategy and resource investment to support the desired lead volume."*

---

*   Pseudonym

The firm pivoted to selling this new offering primarily through an e-commerce channel, but it took a while to build the capabilities to do this successfully. One former executive shared,

> *"We did not fully think through the sales channel conflict implications, such as a lot of the midmarket accounts were part of existing sellers' territories. So we had to decide if we were going to give existing sellers quota retirement for ecommerce sales or were we going to redo territories and build an inside salesforce."*

Furthermore, supporting a competitive e-commerce sales channel took significant investment. The former head of global marketing said,

> *"At the time, we did not appreciate that success in e-commerce depends on the ability to make changes to the digital experience quickly. We were used to working in an environment where web updates were submitted to and prioritized by a centralized digital team, which inevitably took a long time to implement. We struggled to adjust to the fast-paced needs of an e-commerce platform where update frequency and speed were crucial to support a model based on rapid testing and learning.*
>
> *"We were trying to transition from being a high touch, white glove sales organization to an Amazon. We did not have the infrastructure to support it."*

What's the Difference? Target Market versus ICP versus Persona

Before we dive into how to select your target market, let's define a few terms. A target market segment, an ideal customer profile (ICP), and a persona are related concepts in commercialization strategy, but they are not the same thing. Each serves a different purpose in helping businesses focus their commercialization efforts. Here's how they differ:

	Definition	Example
Target Market	A specific group of potential customers within the broader market that a firm has decided to aim its marketing efforts and products toward	Small- to medium-sized enterprises (SMEs) in the technology sector with fifty to two hundred employees
Ideal Customer Profile (ICP)	Detailed description of a fictitious organization that represents the perfect customer for what a company is selling	Technology start-ups that have received Series A funding and are looking to scale their operations efficiently
Persona	A fictional character created to represent a potential buyer and user of the product	"Tech Start-up Steve," a founder of a tech start-up who values efficiency and scalability, struggles with managing disparate tools, and seeks an integrated software solution to streamline operations

In practice, a business might identify *several* target market segments as part of its market strategy and then develop one or more ideal customer profiles to guide its sales and marketing tactics within those segments.

How to Select Your Target Market

Deciding which customer segments to target and defining your ICP is a multistep process that we'll outline across the next few pages. Please note that the steps are mostly the same, regardless of maturity and product strategy, but the emphasis and technique will vary based on where you are in developing the actual product and whether you have validated product-market fit.

For example, while deciding what to build, you may go through a very abbreviated, back-of-the-napkin version of these steps. During discovery/prelaunch, you want to go more in-depth, but you don't have data yet on existing customers/users. Postlaunch but before validating product-market fit, you'll likely have a mix of customers across sub-segments and personas (depending on how narrow you start) as you're figuring out what resonates most, and now you have more data. At product-market fit, you can use this cycle to hone and focus on scaling up.

Step 1. Understand Your Product

Before targeting any customer segment, have a clear understanding of your new solution. This assumes the solution has already started development. If it hasn't, then we recommend prioritizing selecting the most attractive target market segment (s) part of your up-front strategy and before beginning development.

You want to know or have hypotheses for the following:

- What problem does it solve?

- What unique benefits does it offer?

- How does it differentiate from existing solutions?

We also suggest having a theory on how your solution will solve the problem better and/or less expensively than existing solutions and that you use a tool like Tony Ulwick's Jobs-to-be-Done Growth Strategy Matrix[11]:

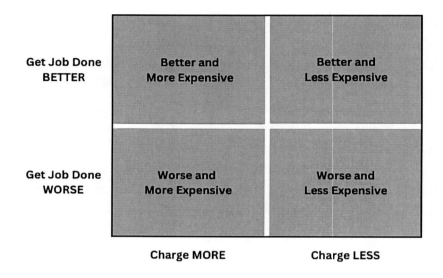

	Charge MORE	Charge LESS
Get Job Done BETTER	Better and More Expensive	Better and Less Expensive
Get Job Done WORSE	Worse and More Expensive	Worse and Less Expensive

Step 2. Identify Potential Segments

Based on your understanding of your product, take a first pass at identifying potential customer segments that might benefit the most from your product. Segments can be defined by various criteria, including demographic, geographic, psychographic, and behavioral factors.

For example, Kainos, a UK-based company, initially started as a provider of IT consulting and services. Kainos had a strong presence in the healthcare sector, and based on their services work, they developed Evolve, a digital platform designed to automate patient records and workflows, making it easier for healthcare providers to access, manage, and share patient information. It identified the following potential market segments:

- **Public Healthcare Institutions**: Recognizing the unique challenges faced by public healthcare systems, such as budget constraints and the need for efficiency, Evolve could offer a cost-effective solution to improve patient care and operational efficiency.

- **Private Healthcare Providers**: Evolve also appealed to private healthcare providers looking for competitive advantages in patient care and operational excellence. By also offering customization and integration capabilities, Kainos could cater to the high expectations of private sector clients.

- **Research and Development Organizations**: Beyond direct patient care, Evolve's data management capabilities made it an attractive solution for organizations involved in healthcare research and development. Kainos could target this segment with features that support data analysis and collaboration on a secure platform.

Step 3. Market Research

Voice of the Customer

Understanding your customers—or more specifically, their urgent and expensive problems*—is the key to successful commercialization of a new product or service. Too many companies waste time developing or positioning a product or service that no one wants or needs.

Ideally, this market research is done prior to the first version of the product being developed and then refreshed on a regular basis

---

* We introduced the concept of "urgent and expensive problems" in our book *Productize*, and it refers to customer problems that ideally need to be addressed in the next twelve months and are important enough to spend money solving. We prefer using "urgent and expensive problems" more than the classic "'jobs-to-be-done" framework when identifying and prioritizing product ideas.

to develop and evolve both the go-to-market strategy and the product roadmap.

Your market research should include both primary research (interviews or surveys with target customers) as well as secondary research looking at factors such as industry growth trends. In our first book, *Productize*, we describe how to do hypothesis-based market research effectively. You can look at those resources here: https://www.vecteris.com/productize-book-tools.

In our experience, the qualitative voice of the customer research yields the most actionable insights than any other research you could do. More than competitive research, market sizing research or even large sample size pricing surveys.

For example, AMEND Consulting created an inventory optimization tool for its clients, who are mostly midmarket industrial companies. They first thought the buyer was the operations leader who wanted to manage inventory, but after a few of the customer interviews, they realized that those individuals cared more about having enough inventory, whereas the CFOs wanted to optimize inventory because it represented cash on the balance sheet. For CFOs, the problem of excess inventory was urgent and expensive, but not so much for operations leaders.

Another great example comes from TenTen Group, a brand implementation firm that has a premium consulting service to help organizations through all the complexities of implementing a rebrand. They hypothesized that they could package their expertise and deliver it to a sub-segment of marketing leaders who couldn't afford the bespoke services. After a little customer research, the target marketing leaders suggested that branding agencies add it as part of their own services. That way it was more likely to be considered up-front and would be in the hands of someone who would know how to use it and provide good guidance.

Competitive Research

You also need to analyze your competitors to understand the markets they are targeting and how. A competitor is any resource serving the same customers and addressing the same problems. A few different types of "non-obvious" competitors include:

1. Inertia as Competition:

    a. Free and "Do Nothing": such as interns, Chat GPT, anything already in the Microsoft suite or Google suite, etc.

    b. Platforms and Incumbents: such as an existing CRM that offers a substandard way to solve the problem but is integrated and free, or an existing service provider that is already in-house and trusted but it's not their specialty.

2. Advanced Internal Capabilities to DIY: more mature customers may have strong internal DIY capabilities.

3. Different Solutions to the Same Problem: such as airline travel versus train travel versus the bus versus the family car.

4. Future Threats: such as, what happens if Amazon decides to enter this space?

Competitive research should include:

*   What is each competitor's value proposition and positioning?

*   What market segments are they targeting, and where do they appear to have the most success?

*   What strategies and channels do they use to market and sell their products or services channels?

*   How do they package and price their products?

- What are their strengths and weaknesses (either from your own knowledge of the product or customer reviews)

- How might they grow in the future?

Again, in our first book, *Productize*, we devote a lot of time to describing how to conduct effective competitive research and encourage you to look at those resources here: *https://www.vecteris.com/productize-book-tools*.

Step 4. Evaluate Segment Attractiveness:

For each potential segment, evaluate its attractiveness based on criteria. The most common criteria are:

1. Size;

2. Growth potential;

3. Accessibility or cost of reaching the segment (i.e., customer acquisition costs); and

4. Profitability, which will be a function of the segment's financial health, willingness to pay, budget, and the competition within the segment.

Attractiveness Criteria 1—Current Size

Sometimes an organization identifies an urgent and expensive problem, but it's because a market segment is too small, too price-sensitive, and/or is not a good fit with their core services. For example, one copywriting services company decided to use their existing internal writing training program for new employees and develop it into a new product that clients could buy to train their own staff. Unfortunately, after spending well into six figures developing the new external-facing program, they found that the only companies interested in the training were the small handful of very large companies with teams of in-house copywriters. The target market for this product was too small.

Other times, one customer's request may be mistaken as representative of the needs of many customers. When this happens, you risk building a product that only one company wants, which only works if they fully fund the development at your average profit margin.

If a segment is too small to yield a strong return with a product developed specifically for them, it's worth exploring the idea of serving that smaller segment with a more generic product and differentiate the marketing messaging for the smaller segment, rather than differentiating the product features for the smaller segment. For example, it may not make economic sense to create an industry-specific version of a product designed for corporate finance departments, but industry-specific marketing messaging for the product could be developed.

Total addressable market (TAM), serviceable available market (SAM), and serviceable obtainable market (SOM) are metrics used to assess the market size and a product's potential for growth within that market.

TAM estimates total demand for a service or product in a market, indicating the maximum market opportunity available. SAM narrows down TAM to the segment of the market that is within your product's reach, considering your current business model and geographical reach. SOM further refines SAM to the portion of the market you can realistically capture in the short term, accounting for competition, market readiness, and other limiting factors.

To use these metrics effectively, start by estimating the TAM to understand the broad market potential. Then, identify your SAM by focusing on the segments you can serve with your current products and distribution channels. Finally, calculate your SOM by evaluating your market share and growth potential within SAM, considering your specific competitive advantages and marketing strategies. Thankfully,

AI tools have made this research much faster than it used to be (just be sure to validate the results).

We prefer to take a bottom-up approach to calculating your SOM by building a list of real prospects and customers. You can typically do this by leveraging existing customer lists and market research and sort it based on likely willingness to buy. This approach tends to yield a much more near-term estimate of revenue potential, and it is much more actionable for the product leader and sales team than just a number.

A more traditional method of calculating market size is the top-down method. For example, when ThoughtWorks, a global software consultancy, developed GoCD, a tool that streamlines the software deployment processes, they started by estimating the **TAM** for GoCD as the global market of all businesses that develop software. This includes a wide range of industries from technology start-ups to software companies to large enterprises with in-house software development teams across the globe.

Considering GoCD's specific features and ThoughtWorks' expertise, they estimated the **SAM** as medium to large technology companies, especially those already adopting Agile and DevOps practices within regions where ThoughtWorks has a strong presence. This segment reflects a more focused market that ThoughtWorks could service with its current business model and product offering.

To estimate the **SOM**, ThoughtWorks considered its competitive advantages, such as their reputation in Agile consulting and competition from other similar tools. The SOM is a realistic target market share within the SAM, factoring in marketing efforts, sales strategies, and the network effect from their existing consulting clients who might adopt GoCD early on.

Attractiveness Criteria 2—Growth Potential

Ideally, we want to target markets that are forecasted to grow both in number and in spending power.

To understand growth potential, look at historical sales data, industry reports, and market research to understand how the market and its segments have grown over time. This can provide a baseline for future growth expectations. Strong sales growth among competitors can indicate a growing market. Consider technological advancements, regulatory changes, and shifts in customer behavior that could influence future growth. For example, ThoughtWorks thought the increasing interest in Agile software development methodologies would drive growth of their SAM.

Attractiveness Criteria 3—Cost to Acquire

A market segment may become unattractive if the costs to acquire customers in that segment are too high. Customer acquisition costs are influenced by things such as existing customer relationships and brand awareness as well as geographic location. Understanding the cost to acquire should include the following:

1. Cost to Create a Lead—How accessible is the customer to your organization? How do you get noticed? Do you have virality?

2. Cost to Convert a Lead—Do you need a professional seller versus product-led? What is the sales cycle length? How many people need to approve the purchase decision?

3. Confidence in 1 and 2 Based on How Well You Know the Customer—Low confidence increases the risk that the cost to acquire is higher than forecasted.

A simple decision is often whether to introduce a new offering to existing customers, new customers within market segments you already serve, or to target entirely new market segments. This decision involves careful consideration of various strategic factors. If the new offering solves an urgent and expensive problem for each segment, each segment will likely have its benefits and challenges.

For example, ThoughtWorks's existing relationships with tech companies and software development communities provided a strong channel to market GoCD. ThoughtWorks's consultancy arm could also cross-sell GoCD to its current clients, leveraging its consultancy projects to introduce the product.

Targeting existing customers leverages established relationships, is cost-effective, and getting immediate feedback on ideas for new offerings or features is typically easier. However, it risks cannibalization, customer confusion, and customer concentration. Targeting new customers within existing markets takes advantage of market familiarity and established channels, as well as brand equity and established proof points. Entering entirely new market segments presents opportunities for growth, diversification, and enhancing the brand's innovative image. However, it involves higher customer acquisition costs as you build brand recognition and a new sales pipeline.

In our experience, it is important to challenge assumptions that existing customers are NOT a good target market before deciding to target new customers or new markets.

Attractiveness Criteria 4—Gross Profitability

A market segment's gross profitability includes willingness to pay and cost to serve/deliver. Understanding the size of existing budgets (purchasing power) and a market segment's experience in solving the problem you address (value perception) are important market research steps. This also includes understanding what competitors are also targeting this market. Some market segments may be underserved or not targeted effectively by competitors, which may provide you with more revenue opportunity.

Also, different segments may have varying service needs and expectations, leading to different costs to serve. A segment that requires high levels of service or expensive customization may not be profitable if those costs exceed the revenue generated from serving them. Understanding the cost to serve ensures that you focus on segments where the business can efficiently deliver value and maintain healthy margins.

For ThoughtWorks, mid- to large-sized tech companies were likely to have higher gross profitability because these companies typically had the budget, complex needs, and strategic desire to invest in tools like GoCD; they had a higher willingness to pay. They also had a higher cost-to-serve with more demanding integration and support requirements, but ThoughtWorks leveraged their core services business to do this work for additional revenue.

The most unattractive segment for ThoughtWorks was rapidly scaling start-ups. While this segment presented exciting opportunities due to their growth potential and need for efficient tools like GoCD to manage their expanding operations, start-ups often operate under significant budget constraints and may have a lower willingness to pay for premium solutions, seeking cost-effective or even free tools to conserve resources instead. They can also require extensive support and customization as they grow and evolve and their requirements change, making the cost to serve high.

Step 5. Prioritize Segments and Communicate

To prioritize segments and communicate their priority to the larger organization, we suggest creating an ICP grid, which visually organizes different segments within your overall ideal customer profile. It helps communicate to others in your firm why you have chosen to concentrate on certain segments and helps focus sales and marketing efforts on the most promising prospects by categorizing potential customers based on various criteria, such as their fit with your product or service and their likelihood to buy.

Start by drawing a grid with two axes representing the criteria you consider most important. For example, one axis might represent the "solution fit" (low to high), and the other could represent "purchase readiness" (low to high).

Then, place different customer segments into the grid based on where they fall along the axes. This visual representation helps you quickly see which segments are your highest priority (e.g., high fit and high readiness) and which are lower priority.

For example, a B2B company that provides cybersecurity solutions tailored for small- to mid-sized financial institutions would plot its segments as follows:

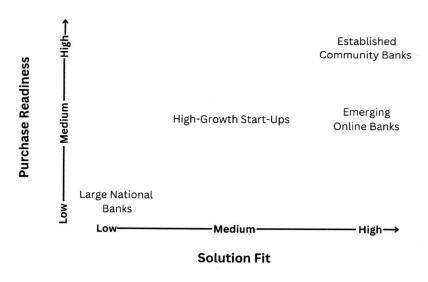

Focus your efforts on the segments in the high-priority quadrant, customizing your messaging, outreach, and engagement strategies to their specific characteristics and needs. The lower-priority segments are cultivated for longer-term engagement or moved to market research. For example, the cybersecurity firm for financial services institutions would:

- Focus Sales Efforts: Prioritize established community banks where their solution fits well and purchase readiness is high, indicating a strong match and a higher likelihood of sales success.

- Tailored Marketing: Develop specific marketing campaigns targeting emerging online banks, emphasizing cost-effectiveness and specialized cybersecurity solutions for digital banks to move them toward higher-purchase readiness.

- Long-Term Engagement: Engage high-growth start-ups with educational content and cybersecurity best practices, nurturing them as they grow and their purchase readiness increases.

- Market Research: For large national banks, conduct further research or product development to better meet their needs or decide to focus efforts elsewhere where the fit and readiness are higher.

Step 6. Develop Segment-Level Targeting Strategies

Based on your analysis, develop a targeting strategy that outlines how you will position your product to appeal to the chosen segment(s). This should include tailored marketing messages, channels, and a value proposition that resonates with the segment.

For example, we worked with a mid-sized environmental compliance consulting firm as they developed a targeting strategy for their new product, an environmental impact assessment software.

First, we helped them identify several key segments within the market that would benefit most from their software:

- **Manufacturing and Industrial**: Businesses in sectors with significant environmental footprints requiring regular compliance with environmental regulations.

- **Construction and Real Estate**: Companies needing to assess environmental impacts as part of project planning and compliance with local regulations.

- **Small and Medium Enterprises (SMEs)**: Smaller businesses seeking cost-effective solutions to meet regulatory compliance without extensive in-house expertise.

We then estimated the size, growth potential, and specific needs of each segment, identifying manufacturing and industrial companies as the highest priority target due to their high need for compliance management and potential environmental impact.

We outlined a mix of digital marketing channels and industry-specific platforms to reach their target segments (a.k.a. "how to reach them"):

- **LinkedIn and Industry Forums**: For direct engagement with decision-makers in manufacturing, construction, and real estate sectors.

- **Content Marketing**: Publishing case studies, whitepapers, and blog posts on their website and through industry publications, highlighting the importance of environmental compliance and the benefits of their software.

- **Trade Shows and Conferences**: Participating in industry-specific events to showcase their software and network with potential clients.

For each segment, we tailored the value proposition for the impact assessment software (a.k.a. "what to say to them"):

- **Manufacturing and Industrial**: Highlighting the software's ability to manage and mitigate risks associated with environmental compliance, thereby avoiding fines and facilitating sustainable operations.

- **Construction and Real Estate**: Focusing on the software's capability to streamline environmental impact assessments for projects, ensuring compliance and speeding up approval processes.

- **SMEs**: Emphasizing ease of use, affordability, and the ability to ensure compliance without the need for dedicated environmental compliance staff.

By thoroughly understanding their market, carefully selecting target segments, and then tailoring their marketing and sales strategies to meet the specific needs of those segments, the firm could better reach and resonate with prospective customers actively seeking environmental compliance solutions.

Step 7. Operationalize ICP Into Sales Process (a.k.a. Lead Management)

You will need to decide who will own screening leads against your ICP to focus sellers on the best prospective customers. In many organizations, inbound lead generation and initial qualification will sit with marketing, but there also needs to be a sales function that is helping sellers talk to the right leads at the right time. The sellers may reach out to leads, nurturing them with targeted communications and scheduling, or, as your business matures, you may decide to invest in creating a sales development representative role (SDR). We'll talk more about SDRs in chapter 5.

Even if you are selling to existing customers, you'll be much more successful if you carefully choose WHO you are going to sell to rather than just "shaking the opportunity tree and seeing what falls out."

For example, one product leader who recently launched a new product designed to be cross-sold to existing customers shared,

> *"I used to think prospect list management was so annoying. But in this last product launch, we were successful because we took the time to understand the account dynamics at a line-by-line level. We knew where there was an easy upgrade opportunity and where we may be able re-engage clients based on this new product. We had a hypothesis for each opportunity on why they might buy. We also had to look at the competencies of the seller who owned each opportunity to see who would need extra support. I'm convinced that developing and managing the list of prospects and deciding who we were going to talk to and why they might buy was the most important and hardest thing we did."*

This product leader's experience underscores how important it is to carefully choose your first wave of target customers. Be deliberate about your early customer target list so you can achieve the most success for the least amount of effort. For example, you might target customers who were part of your initial market research or who are newer to the role and perhaps more innovative in their thinking or open to experimentation. They could also just be prospects that are in the territories of your strongest sellers who are most excited about productization. The success of the early sales efforts will generate more enthusiasm for the productization strategy and provide seller and client case studies to help persuade others of the benefit.

Step 8. Iterate and Adapt

The market is dynamic. Customer preferences and competitive landscapes can change. That's why it is important to continuously monitor the performance of your product within your target segments and be ready to adapt your strategy as necessary.

For example, we suggest reviewing your win-loss data on a quarterly basis. Who you "win" will be a good indicator of who your ICP is.

We also suggest refreshing your competitor analysis quarterly and consider tracking metrics that speak to:

- Company health, that is, changes in company size (revenue and employees), changes in primary investors, new patents, etc.
- Key product performance metrics from the customer perspective (price, quality, delivery, ease of use)
- New product launches
- Marketing strategies, that is, content channels and content quality

We also suggest regularly refreshing your customer research. One of the easiest ways to do this is to have a customer advisory board. Gather individuals you think will provide honest opinions, and use the focus group dynamic of an advisory board meeting to solicit feedback and develop ideas. Set criteria for who is included (such as long-term customers or customers who buy at a certain level), or strategic invitations can go out to people projected to provide valuable insights.

Data such as website traffic, lead generation sources, and conversion rates by segment should also be monitored.

Target Market Selection Dos and Don'ts

In addition to following a process to select your target market(s) and ICP(s), we've identified a few "dos and don'ts" for B2B services firms who are developing new solutions and products. Depending on your maturity, they are:

Maturity Stages 0–1: Discovery and Validating Product-Market Fit

1. Do go "uncomfortably" narrow

2. Don't add new verticals too early

3. Do mitigate cannibalization risk

Maturity Stages 2–3: Validating Product-Market Fit and Scaling

4. Do know and speak to the buyers and stakeholders at the ICP

5. Do target "in-market" prospects

The Value of Going "Uncomfortably" Narrow

We love the adage, *"The riches are in the niches."*

Or another one, *"A product for everyone is a product that is for no one."*

While it may be tempting to go broad, especially as you are still trying to figure out product-market fit or go-to-market fit, it makes it much harder to quickly learn what is working about your product and go-to-market approach and what is not. In early maturity, we like the advice to go "uncomfortably" narrow and prioritize the narrowest niche that you can and then test with the market segment quickly so that you know whether to keep going or to select a different segment. We appreciate the natural tension between this advice and the inclination to attack a large SOM and TAM. It's why every start-up has a

HUGE TAM, but because they try to sell to everyone, they wind up not having a path to anywhere. Our advice is to find a niche in an attractive TAM and be strategic about the sequence of niches you will target so that you "unlock" the TAM.

John Riley, the chief commercial officer of a SaaS start-up in the sales intelligence space, was working to transform the company from one that manually matched clients with sales intelligence "experts" to one where clients could self-serve, and search, match, and schedule with these experts using an online platform. John shared,

> *"Our first task was to home in on ICP. We had been using a pretty shotgun scatter approach to defining our target market and said we would serve all tech companies.*
>
> *I started by looking at our existing clients, and we identified five narrow niches where we had the most success: security, data analytics, IT infrastructure, IT management software, and cloud. Then we identified the buying personas for each niche and aligned our sales resources to those markets. But we had to narrow our ICP before we could do anything else."*

By targeting a specific segment and ICP, companies deploy their resources more effectively, concentrating efforts on prospects with the highest conversion potential and leading to more efficient marketing spend and a higher ROI on sales.

A deep understanding of a narrow target market and ICP enables companies to clearly articulate how their solutions outperform their competitors. This clarity enhances competitive advantage.

Also, if you identify and target an underserved niche, you can establish a strong presence and brand loyalty more swiftly and get market penetration before exploring broader markets.

Don't Add New Verticals Too Early[12]

Adding new verticals (i.e., additional target market segments) too early can stretch resources thin and lead to a lack of depth in any given market. It is better to focus on a narrow target segment or ICP to build strong expertise, tailor your product or service closely to customer needs, and establish a solid market presence before expanding.

Deeply understanding one segment takes time. Spreading efforts across multiple segments too soon can prevent you from developing the deep insights needed to successfully tailor your go-to-market approach for each segment.

Mitigate Cannibalization Risk

Fear of cannibalizing current services or products can kill our best products before they even have a chance to succeed. If you are to be successful, you must address any cannibalization fears and move past them, and there are ways, especially early, to mitigate the risk of cannibalization.

To mitigate the impact of cannibalization, perform a side-by-side comparison of the personas and problems of current customer segments with the new customer segments to see how much overlap exists. If most of the attributes overlap, your new product may cannibalize part of your existing revenue. If the circles are mutually exclusive, then the new product is unlikely to cannibalize.

For example, if you are creating a feature-light product offered at a lower price point to attract a more cost-conscious customer, there likely won't be much overlap between the customer segments. For example, Empower, a creative media agency, created MediaAgent, a SaaS-based media planning tool for smaller companies who cannot afford, or need, the more bespoke media planning work Empower does for large clients. MediaAgent uses data to help companies plan and buy advertising across television, radio, and digital platforms.

There is little concern about cannibalization because MediaAgent is geared toward smaller clients who need less support and who aren't willing to pay as much.

Just keep in mind that despite tactics like this, we also advise organizations, especially with the recent advancements in AI, to be prepared for some disruption and be open to the risk of cannibalization.

Know and Speak to the Buyers and Stakeholders at the ICP

It's important not just to outline the target market segment and ICP but to also identify the potential buying personas because different buyers may require different messaging. For example, a CFO might be focused on ROI and cost savings, while an IT manager may prioritize technical capabilities and integration. If you focus only on the end users of your product without considering the other buyers or buyer stakeholders (e.g., CFO or procurement team), your value proposition may not address their cost-benefit concerns, leading to stalled or lost deals. We see this a lot with companies producing technical content that appeals to IT staff but neglects the business impact and fails to engage business stakeholders.

When TalentTether* expanded its offerings beyond outplacement services to include upskilling products, it realized it opened many more potential buying personas. The firm's chief marketing officer shared, *"We assumed our buyer was only HR. But there were a lot of buyers out there managing lines of business."*

In essence, while identifying the target market segment and ICP is foundational, failing to also understand and cater to the specific buyer personas within these segments—each with their own set of concerns, criteria, and influence on the purchasing process—can lead to ineffective marketing, misaligned sales strategies, and ultimately, missed opportunities for closing deals and fostering long-term customer relationships.

---

*   Pseudonym

Target the "In-Market" ICP

The in-market ICP is a highly detailed description of a customer or business that is actively seeking solutions, showing readiness to buy, and matches the characteristics of your solution's ideal customer.

It adds an additional layer of intent and timing into the mix, focusing on prospects that are not just a fit in terms of attributes and needs but are also *in the market* for your product or service right now.

To define an in-market ICP, you should combine your usual ICP criteria (such as company size, industry, budget, and specific needs) with indicators of *purchase intent*. These indicators might include recent actions that suggest a readiness to buy, such as:

- Visiting specific pages on your website (e.g., pricing or product comparison pages)
- Engaging with your content or ads related to purchasing decisions
- Downloading buying guides or product specs
- Participating in webinars or online demos
- Asking detailed questions about features, implementation, or pricing through direct contact channels

Focusing on in-market ICPs allows you to concentrate efforts on prospects who are most likely to convert in the near term, thereby increasing efficiency and potentially improving the conversion rate.

Get the Core "White Hot": a.k.a. Select Your Pilots Carefully

One of the most important decisions you will make in early maturity is which market segment to pilot with. Sometimes called a closed beta, you'll use this pilot to refine messaging, pricing, and demand generation tactics.

In addition to selecting an attractive market segment, you'll need to think carefully about the types of customers you are most likely to succeed with and least likely to disrupt other businesses within your organization. You'll want to be very deliberate about the markets (regional, national) and the teams (sales and/or delivery) that you pilot with, so you get the most support with the least friction.

For example, if you are introducing a productized solution that might compete with or cannibalize traditional services, you may decide to pilot with an industry market segment where you don't currently have a lot of existing customers so that there is less internal resistance to marketing and selling it. For example, AMEND Consulting is targeting highly regulated, COGS heavy businesses for its inventory optimization tool. Those aren't great customers for their core inventory management consulting services, so there is little risk of cannibalization of services revenue.

Or if you are introducing a product that works best when bundled with traditional services, you may want to pilot with a seller who has a strong track record of selling bundled solutions and is excited about the new offering.

A successful pilot with a subset of the market is extremely important for services companies who are productizing and need to win the hearts and minds of internal skeptics. The success of the initial pilot will generate more enthusiasm for the productization strategy and provide seller and client case studies to help persuade others of the benefit. Demonstrating that you are learning from the market along the way and making changes as you get more market feedback also helps increase internal enthusiasm.

As you move from the pilot phase, we recommend staging a release to new market segments to further ensure success and focus. Ideally, the early markets are so successful that other market leaders in the organization will start asking "when can we start selling?" the new product rather than having it shoved down their throats.

One product leader of a global HR services company shared with us,

> *"I was very deliberate about the order in which we released the new product to new countries. I focused first on where I knew I would get investment from the regional marketing and delivery teams and where I had buy-in about the market opportunity. I picked my first four markets and told every other market leader to back off so I could focus on the early markets."*

Another product leader compared a successful pilot to "getting the core white-hot." He shared,

> *"You don't want to suffocate a new product in the early days, so I have one top salesperson dedicated to it, and they can sell across all of the territories. She still needs to coordinate with the other sellers, but she can sell in anyone's territory. We cherry-pick the initial list for her to chase based on our hypothesis about the most ideal customer profile. This gives us incredible focus out of the gate to see if the new product has legs."*

Key Takeaways

1. Deciding WHO the best target market is for your new solution is the most important go-to-market decision you'll make because it influences everything else. Decisions about pricing, packaging, positioning, marketing channels, and sales channels all start with your target market.

2. Understanding your customers—or more specifically, their urgent and expensive problems—is the key to successful commercialization of a new product or service. Too many

companies waste time developing or positioning a product or service that no one wants or needs.

3. Sometimes an organization identifies an urgent and expensive problem, but it's in relation to a market segment that is too small, too price-sensitive, and/or is not a good fit with their core services.

4. A market segment may become unattractive if the costs to acquire customers in that segment are too high. Customer acquisition costs are influenced by things such as existing customer relationships and brand awareness as well as geographic location. Understanding the cost to acquire should include both the cost to create a lead and the cost to convert a lead.

5. The market is dynamic. Customer preferences and competitive landscapes can change. That's why it is important to continuously monitor the performance of your product within your target segments and adapt your strategy as necessary.

6. Go "uncomfortably narrow" and prioritize the narrowest niche that you can, and then test with the market segment quickly so that you know whether to keep going or to select a different segment.

7. Adding new verticals (i.e., additional target market segments) too early can stretch resources thin and lead to a lack of depth in any given market.

8. One of the most important decisions you will make in early maturity is which market segment(s) to pilot with. In addition to selecting an attractive market segment, you'll need to think carefully about the types of customers you are most likely to succeed with and the teams within your organization that will

be involved in the pilot (sales and/or delivery) where you get the most support with the least friction.

Additional Resources

✕ Customer interview guidelines and questions

✕ Persona identification worksheet

✕ Sample interview deck and questions

✕ Sample survey questions

✕ Customer advisory board creation checklist

✕ Competitor research checklist and guidelines

✕ Competitor comparison grid and analysis templates

✕ In-Market ICP vs. Regular ICP attributes

✕ Example market segment attractiveness & ICP grids

(Please download the tools at www.commercializebook.com)

CHAPTER 3

MONETIZE NEW OFFERINGS (A.K.A. PRICING AND PACKAGING)

One commercial real estate services firm that we work with manages millions of square feet for enterprises around the globe. The traditional model the firm uses to price their real estate management services is cost-plus. This pricing strategy has worked well for them because it is a price sensitive industry, and the strategy mitigates the economic risk of hundreds of embedded facilities managers performing myriad tasks for their clients.

The chief product officer recognized that as they prepared to launch innovative new products such as energy efficiency management software or EV chargers to offer alongside their standard management services, it was not just the technology that needed to change, but the business model as well. The CPO has passionately led the charge to get her team to think differently about how they monetize their offerings to make sure they are properly rewarded for the unique value the products bring to customers.

Not just thinking inwardly about the costs and desired margins, but how the customers perceive the value was an important mindset shift. This didn't mean becoming more expensive. The firm has a goal to fundamentally change the cost curve for customers in the industry. But it has meant changing how they think about creating value and being rewarded for that.

In making this shift, this real estate services firm has avoided one of the most common mistakes we see when organizations package and price their productized services or products: setting prices by simply adding a markup to forecasted costs and missing the opportunity to align prices to customer value.

Other common mistakes we see include:

1. Not aligning pricing to the product strategy.

2. Not researching or testing pricing. This includes not interviewing or surveying customers to test perceived value and willingness to pay by customer segment. Or maybe the organization conducts a little research but does not run tests with real customers before a broad rollout. This mistake can also include ignoring competitor or industry dynamics.

3. Setting the same price for all customers and not using complexity to price discriminate between customer segments that have a different willingness to pay.

4. Setting the price too low and/or not raising prices. This often happens because organizations are still anchored to a cost-plus model and underestimate the willingness of customers to pay for the value.

Why We Call this "Monetizing"

The strategies you use to create packages, determine how prices will be calculated, and set price points are the cornerstones for enjoying sustainable high-profit margins[13]. Often, when we are asked to help an organization determine the pricing and packaging for their new products or productized services, we discover that they have not fully thought through how the new offering will create more profits for the organization. Yes, "more customers, lower costs" is part of their profit model, but it is far from that simple.

For example, when the commercial real estate services firm developed its new products, it pivoted to selling a fundamentally new offering. They were no longer selling people's time and expertise as boots on the ground to manage a facility but a packaged solution that included their services plus an unparalleled data set, hardware and software technology products that work in concert, and unique expertise. The business model needed to change as well.

The terms "business model," "distribution model," and "pricing model" are often used in the context of your product's strategy, but they refer to different aspects of how the product generates revenue.

A **business model** outlines the framework of how a product creates, delivers, and captures value. It encompasses the company's plan for making a profit, detailing the products or services it will sell, its target market, and any expected costs. The business model is a holistic view of the company's strategy for operating within its ecosystem. It includes how it engages with customers, the value proposition, key resources, partnerships, revenue streams, investments in fixed/intangible assets, cost structure, and competitive advantage.

The **distribution model** is the net profit over the lifetime of the customer less the cost to acquire the customer.

A **pricing model** is a component of the business model that specifically focuses on the strategy for setting the price of the company's products or services. It influences the net profit part of the distribution model calculation. It outlines how a company will charge its customers, considering factors like production costs, market demand, competitor pricing, and value perception.

Organizations cannot determine a pricing model until they articulate how the new products or productized services support and/or change their existing business model and how the products will be distributed. Often this step is skipped or underdeveloped at the beginning of the business decision to productize and regrettably must be revisited when a product is ready to go to market.

Most B2B Services Organizations Struggle to Adopt Value-Based Pricing Models

Most products are priced on the value they deliver, but value-based pricing can be foreign for many B2B professional services firms who often tailor their services to each client's specific needs and frequently use time and materials or cost-plus pricing.

Pricing based on value delivered rather than the time it takes to deliver value is a significant mindset shift. For example, time/materials and cost-plus may appear to be less risky. Too often, organizations are overly concerned with protecting from downside risk and end up missing out on much bigger upside potential.

It requires a different way of thinking and a new set of skills to standardize offerings and pricing. If we are selling to existing customers, they may also be anchored to hours/services-based pricing. Clients may struggle to determine the true value of the services they receive, further complicating the pricing strategy. The new model needs to feel advantageous to them.

Input 1—Product Strategy and How It Ties to the Business Strategy

At its essence, your product strategy and how it ties to the business strategy should answer the question "How are we going to make more profits than our competition"?[14]

Many organizations do not clearly think through this question.

To start, it helps to define what you are pricing and the strategic goals of what you are pricing.

What are you pricing? For example, is it a . . .

- standalone product
- bundled product
- complementary product
- add-on
- new pricing tier (with added features)
- price increase

What are the strategic goals of what you are pricing? For example, is it to be a loss leader for more profitable parts of the business to maximize product adoption or to maximize retention?

For example, Employee Navigator, which is now one of the leading benefits administration platforms in the US, saw a trend of new tech start-ups entering the industry and looking to bypass a key channel partner, the health broker industry. Employee Navigator made the strategic decision to go the other direction and become the most broker-friendly SaaS benefits administration platform. To support this strategy, they changed their pricing model from the industry standard per employee per month to an enterprise license that better incentivized brokers to put as much of their book of business on the platform as possible. By moving to an enterprise-license model, brokers could put an unlimited number of businesses and employees on the platform at no extra cost.

And it worked.

In a matter of just a few years, they added millions of employees to the platform. Then, they added very small per-employee-per-month data integration charges and exchange fees—not to the brokers, but to the insurance carriers, who realized the value of higher data quality to their own businesses. Once Employee Navigator attracted a high volume of employees to the platform by making it super cheap for the main channel partner (brokers), they knew there would be many other ways to monetize access to employees.

Making a preliminary decision about whether something is a new standalone product, part of a larger bundle, etc. should happen early before the product starts to be developed when you are defining the value proposition. If it is going to be sold as part of a bundle or a complementary product, then you'll want to know what role it will play in driving revenue for other parts of the business, and your pricing strategy will need to consider that impact.

Similarly, making a preliminary decision for the market positioning of the new offering should also happen before development. By market positioning, we mean whether you going to be a low-cost provider or a high-quality solution. The more competitive the market you are in, the more important it is to be very clear on whether you are competing on price, on product quality, or even on sales (e.g., having a low or no-touch sales process), and this decision has a significant impact on how you think about pricing[15].

If the product is sold to the same market as your current offerings, especially if it is going to be bundled or complements current offerings, the market positioning for the new offering should align to the market positioning of your current offerings and brand promise.

Kristen Howe, chief product officer of Linkage, a leadership development company, explained why market positioning was so important to their pricing strategy.

> *"We were not a low-cost provider, but the pricing did not reflect that positioning. Before we standardized pricing, our pricing was too low for the quality of our product and the market position we wanted to occupy. It was hard to teach our team to have pricing integrity so we would not come across as a low-cost provider. It's been several years now, and we still have legacy*

customers we are migrating up to our new standardized pricing because they've resisted."

For organizations that are pursuing the strategy of creating separate, standalone product-as-a-service businesses, we also recommend thinking through what Ulrik Lehrskov-Schmidt calls "scale economics" in his excellent book *The Pricing Roadmap*. He explains that a competitive SaaS business model needs to be better in one or all of the following[16]:

Customer acquisition cost (CAC). This is driven by distribution effects and virality. For professional services firms, will this be bundled with services engagements, or will it be an easy cross-sell to existing customers? Do your users do the selling for you? For example, KNIME provides both free open-source data analytics software used by data scientists and private installations and customizations of the software to large multinationals. It generates leads from users of its free open-source software who are employees of large organizations and want their company to start using it. This allows KNIME to sell to large corporations at a fraction of the cost compared to its competitors, who spend months if not years meeting with internal teams up and down the ladder to build a business case for purchase[17]. Their CAC is lower.

Price. The value your product creates drives price. A higher price is driven by factors such as unique expertise, proprietary technology, brand reputation, and exceptional customer service.

A great example is Nielsen, who offers productized market research and data analytics services tailored to specific industries, such as retail, FMCG (fast-moving consumer goods), and media. Nielsen's services are standardized to some extent, offering subscription-based access to comprehensive market reports, consumer behavior insights, and analytics platforms. These productized offerings allow clients to access valuable market insights without the need for custom research projects. Nielsen's competitive advantage lies in its extensive data collection networks, proprietary analytics tools, and deep industry expertise, enabling it to charge premium prices for its productized services.

For some products, premium pricing might be driven by network effects—the more users you have, the more valuable the product is. For example, a membership model creates more network effects that you can then charge a premium for. Another example is American Express, which capitalizes on network effects by fostering a closed-loop system that connects affluent cardholders with businesses. Its high-spending customer base attracts merchants willing to pay higher transaction fees for access to this lucrative segment, enhancing the card's utility and desirability. The more merchants who accept American Express, the more affluent cardholders will use it. Consequently, American Express justifies premium pricing for both cardholders and merchants, leveraging its brand and network.

Unit cost. This is driven by economies of scale. The more productized your solution, the lower it costs to deliver it to one more customer. Build once, sell a thousand times. The marginal cost decreases the more productized it is. But typically to productize, you need more up-front investment.

It is important to understand which strategy you are going to use because it will impact your pricing strategy. For example, if you are relying on network effects to make your product valuable, you may want a freemium (free trial) model. Similarly, if you want individual users to generate leads for large enterprise customers, then a freemium pricing model for individual users may also make sense. Or it may be better to have a "land and expand" strategy with cheap starter prices and quickly raise them after critical mass is reached[18].

Other questions to consider as part of defining your business and product strategy, if you have not already, include:

1. Are there new target segments in the market for the product? If so, what impact will this have on pricing (e.g., value-driven pricing for entry-level targets who are just getting started)?

2. Are there any legal or government regulations relevant to pricing to consider?

3. What are the factors that could impact demand for the product in the coming months/years? How should pricing be affected, if at all?

4. How are current market conditions (inflation, etc.) impacting spend toward similar products right now? How do we anticipate this changing in the short-term?

Input 2—Value to Customers and Willingness to Pay

Good product pricing is grounded in the economic value the product creates for the customer's organization. This starts with understanding the key factors that drive economic value such as:

1. Increases revenue
2. Increases productivity
3. Decreases cost
4. Reallocates cost from one cost center to another
5. Reduces risk/exposure to bad outcomes
6. Reduced uncertainty

To truly understand the value and how it might vary by customer segment, you need to get feedback from customers on their challenges, goals, and how the new solution can help them achieve these goals.

This is a good opportunity to validate the urgent and expensive problem(s) that the solution is designed to solve.

Ask questions to assess what the economic value might be, such as:

- What is the problem currently costing you in money or resources?

- Is solving this problem in your budget?

- On a scale of one to five, how valuable would it be to you to solve this? Why?

- What value would solving this problem have for your company?

This will help you assess potential customers' willingness to pay (WTP). WTP is the maximum amount a consumer is prepared to spend on a good or service. It captures how much value a consumer places on a product, determining the highest price they would agree to for its purchase before deciding to forgo it.

Ask simple questions to assess WTP such as:

- How much would you expect to pay? Why?

- Have you bought something similar in the past? If so, how much did it cost?

- What is your reaction to this proposed pricing?

Asking what a customer expects to pay is very important before showing proposed pricing. If the customer is "anchored*" to a particular price either because of past purchasing experience or the size of the budget allocated to solve the problem, you will want to know that

---

* Anchoring is a concept from behavioral economics that explains why people base an estimate or judgment based on the first piece of information that we receive and then adjust that starting point with new information.

anchor so you can undercut or match it if you decide to use different price points[19].

Then there are different methodologies to test price sensitivity. For example, the Gabor-Granger technique, named after the economists who developed it André Gabor and Clive J. Granger, is a market research method used for determining price elasticity and consumers' willingness to pay for a product or service. By presenting customers with a product and asking if they would purchase it at various price points, the technique gauges the likelihood of purchase at different prices by asking questions such as:

"Would you buy this data set at X price?" Then,

1. If they say yes, the same question is asked with a higher price point.

2. If they say no, the same question is asked with a lower price point.

3. This continues until the model determines the highest price they are willing to pay.

We also like the Van Westendorp technique developed by Dutch economist Peter Van Westendorp. It gauges customers' perceptions of value and their price preferences by asking four specific questions to determine at what price a product is considered too expensive, too cheap, cheap but still considered good value, and getting expensive but still considered worth buying. This provides price ranges and helps pinpoint an optimal price point that balances consumer willingness to pay with perceived product value.

You can learn this customer information through different methods:

1. Customer Interviews: Conduct one-on-one interviews with existing or potential clients to gather qualitative insights on pricing perceptions and willingness to pay.

2. Surveys: Use different types of surveys, such as conjoint analysis, Van Westendorp's Price Sensitivity Meter, or Gabor-Granger technique, to collect quantitative data on clients' preferences and price sensitivity.

3. Charter (Pilot) Programs: Offer your services at different price points to a select group of clients and measure their reactions, satisfaction levels, and purchase behavior. This data can help you refine your pricing strategy.

For example, a B2B market research firm we worked with shifted from custom research projects to offering standardized industry reports in sectors like healthcare and technology to scale its business effectively. They priced the standardized reports by first identifying how its market analysis created value across different client segments. For example, the technology company customers valued insights into emerging trends for prioritizing R&D investments, getting more return on R&D spend. However, their healthcare sector clients used the market research to analyze regulatory environments and understand patient demographics to bring new treatments to market more effectively. Through direct client interviews and surveys, the firm created sample pricing that correlated prices with the perceived value and benefits, and then tested customers' willingness to pay by customer segment.

We believe that willingness to pay, especially early in a product's maturity, is more important than margin protection. One CEO described it as follows:

> *"I think a lot of people get wrapped around the axle using a margin protection pricing strategy, which is not wrong in the long-term, but it's not the right thing to focus on out of the gate. Instead, focus on what people will pay. And make sure you validate that the amount that they are willing to pay is enough to make your TAM, SAM, and SOM worth it. Margin*

protection is meaningless if the overall revenue opportunity is too small."

That said, a high-level estimate of the likely costs required to deliver the product is another input into crafting initial pricing.

Input 3—Costs to Deliver, Sell, and Renew the Product

Most people are pretty good at figuring out delivery costs, especially if you have been pricing your existing services and solutions based on cost-plus. The trickier part is also including customer acquisition and customer retention costs as new and different go-to-market capabilities are likely needed.

For example, how much needs to be spent on promoting this product? For example, if we lean more on earned media, it allows for greater margins and can provide greater flexibility in pricing. How much customer service, implementation support, and account management support are needed to drive expansion and renewal, and what will that cost?

Also, even if the product is going to be a loss leader, you still need to estimate how much of a loss it will be.

Estimating costs can typically be done with known information already available. They fall into two categories:

Direct costs—These can be traced directly to costs to deliver a product or service for a customer or project. They are typically easy to assign and are variable (as you add more customers, these costs increase). Examples include:

- Direct Labor

- Direct Materials

- Commissions

- License Fees

- Cost of Sale
- Cost of Retention

Indirect costs—These can NOT be traced back to a specific product, service, or customer (or require certain assumptions to assign such as allocating based on the percent of total new clients each year). Examples include:

- General & Administrative (G&A) Salaries
- Depreciation
- Utilities and Rent
- Cloud Hosting Fees
- Brand Marketing

After allocating all costs, you can determine the price ranges necessary to achieve the desired margins.

For example, one IT consulting firm we work with ventured into the financial services sector without fully accounting for the unique costs, such as heightened regulatory compliance, increased insurance rates, and specialized staff training. They underpriced their solution, significantly impacting profit margins. Their COO reflected on the experience, *"It seemed like a strategic move, but we quickly learned the hard way that we overlooked the compliance costs and talent premiums and had underpriced the offering."*

Input 4—Competition

Finally, it's important that you know where your competitors are pricing their similar products or solutions.

But it's not enough to just know their prices for different packages. You must understand their value proposition including features, benefits, and differentiators as well as tiered pricing, discounts, and additional fees. It's also important to understand their pricing strategy. For example, are they bundling products together or offering discounts? Are they trying to be the low-cost option in the market or the premium provider?

All these things need to be considered as you price your product so that you don't UNDER price your product so much that it diminishes its value in the eyes of your customers, or OVER price yourself right out of the market. Keep in mind the context in which competitors are operating in such as market conditions, target customer segments, and regional differences, which can all impact pricing strategies.

This research should include:

- Published pricing from competitors' websites, industry reports, and product review sources. This may also help you to understand their value proposition and pricing strategy.

- Customers and prospect interviews, asking some of the value and willingness to pay questions:

  - What have you paid in the past for similar solutions?

  - Are you aware of organizations providing solutions? Do you know what they charge?

  - What does solving this problem cost you now?

While competitor prices are a critical benchmark, don't base your pricing strategy solely on them. Your costs, unique value proposition, and business goals should also significantly influence your pricing decisions. Once you have all these inputs, you are ready to design the pricing and packaging.

Design Pricing and Packing

To help you consider all the building blocks or levers you must pull in your pricing and packaging, we like to use a modified version of the pricing design flow structure from Ulrik Lehrskov-Schmidt's book *The Pricing Roadmap*. Please note that our modified version is for less mature products (before scaling). The building blocks include:

1. Different **packaging** of features and benefits mapped to different submarket segment needs.

2. **Add-ons** mapped to different submarket segment needs.

3. The **price calculation model** that includes the measures and values used to determine the price (e.g., number of employees, plants, seat licenses, etc.).

4. The different **price points** for each configuration.

For example, we worked with an environmental consulting company that helped manufacturing plants be more energy efficient. They developed a productized solution that included assessments, analysis, and monitoring software. They had three different customer segments who all had the same overarching problem to solve—become more energy efficient—but had slightly different desired outcomes. The three segments were heavy manufacturing (urgent and expensive problem is reducing high energy costs,) precision manufacturing (urgent and expensive problem is ensuring energy efficiency without compromising quality), and sustainable manufacturing (urgent and expensive problem is reducing their carbon footprint significantly).

The different urgent and expensive problems for each segment impact their WTP and price sensitivity*.

Packages

This environmental consulting firm developed different packages mapped to the different needs of their segments:

---

* WTP is based on a specific price. Sensitivity is dynamic and measures how much WTP changes based on a change in price.

- **Basic Package:** Designed for small precision manufacturers, offering basic energy monitoring and efficiency recommendations. The focus is on accessibility with a competitive entry price point.

- **Advanced Package:** Aimed at heavy manufacturers, this package includes advanced analytics, predictive maintenance for energy systems, and integration with industrial automation tools.

- **Sustainability Package:** For sustainable manufacturers, offering comprehensive carbon footprint tracking, regulatory compliance modules, and sustainability reporting tools.

The packages are designed to "price the customer." They are packages of value that match the urgent and expensive problems for each segment.

The product value matrix based on early voice of the customer interviews can help inform what features of your solution should be standard versus premium[20].

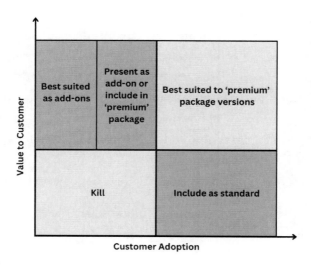

Add-Ons

Additionally, they created a suite of add-ons to the packages that also mapped to the customer segment value propositions. For example, custom integration with existing ERP systems, which was most attractive to the heavy manufacturing segment, and consultancy services for sustainability certification, which was most interesting to sustainable manufacturing.

Pricing Calculation Model

For the pricing calculation model, all packages are offered on an annual subscription basis with the price adjusted not just by the features in that package but also according to plant size and energy consumption.

Selecting an appropriate measure to base the subscription price on involves aligning with the value delivered to the customer while considering operational scalability and fairness. This firm found that a blend of plant size (measured by square footage) and energy consumption (measured in kilowatt-hours, kWh) provided a balanced and equitable basis for determining subscription prices. The size of the manufacturing plant correlates with the potential energy usage and the complexity of implementing energy efficiency solutions (i.e., larger plants require more extensive setup and monitoring points). Directly linking part of the pricing to energy consumption underscores the value proposition of the solution, helping manufacturers reduce energy costs. By choosing this dual measure for subscription pricing, the pricing is scalable and directly tied to the value customers can expect to derive from the product.

To simplify the pricing model for sales, they created tiers:

- Standard: For plants up to 50,000 square feet and consuming up to 500,000 kWh/year.

- Professional: For plants between 50,001 and 100,000 square feet and consuming 500,001–1,000,000 kWh/year.

- Enterprise: For plants over 100,000 square feet or consuming more than 1,000,000 kWh/year.

By aligning the subscription tiers within each package, this firm ensures that its offerings are scalable and adaptable, allowing customers to select a service level that best matches their operational size, energy consumption, and specific needs—whether focused on basic energy efficiency, advanced manufacturing integration, or sustainability goals. Most importantly, it allows the firm to capture value across different market segments.

Here is a visualization of the building blocks:

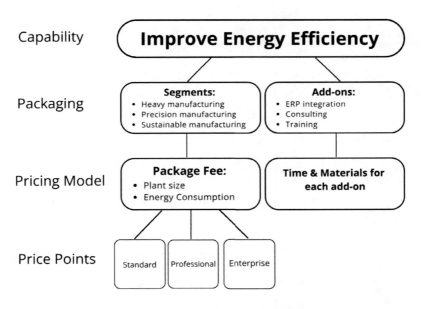

At the very beginning, you may only pursue one market segment. This firm started with heavy manufacturing, because that was where it had the most experience, and then later expanded into small precision manufacturers. It also realized that some of the heavy manufacturers had goals to be world class in sustainability and carved them off into a new market segment—sustainable manufacturers.

As your product matures, you may also decide to expand into a very different type of market segment with a very different problem to solve. For example, if the environmental consulting firm decided it wanted to start serving government agencies whose urgent and expensive problem was not improving energy efficiency at their plants but, instead, assessing the energy efficiency of facilities that they regulate, that would need a completely different pricing model.

Let's dive more into nuances for the three different levels: packaging, price calculation model, and price points.

Packaging

Packages help you "price the customer." They are bundles of value that match both the jobs-to-be-done and the willingness to pay for each segment.

Done well, packages are also an opportunity for you to demonstrate your organization's unique point of view about how your customers' problem presents in different ways and how you have a nuanced understanding of their needs. This is incredibly important for B2B services organizations that are productizing. You will likely have internal resistance to productizing and moving away from a customized offering, and you may also have resistance from existing customers. But packages tailored to the needs of different segments give you an opportunity to show how your offering is still relevant to unique needs. **Well-designed packages can tell a powerful story about how your offering is better than a customized service.**

For example, when Strategy Execution, a premium provider of project management training known for customized, cutting-edge content and learning experiences, decided to launch a subscription-based digital training product, it needed to design its packages and pricing in a way that preserved its market positioning. The first way the firm signaled to the market that its more productized offering was a premium-product was by creating packages for different types of users.

Matthew Ansbro, former chief revenue officer of Strategy Execution, shared,

> *"We curated packages for certain roles and disciplines, which signaled to the market that we had given a lot of thought about how the learning needs of a Project Manager may be different from the learning needs of a product manager. Tailoring packages for different users gave our sellers more credibility that the solution was thoughtfully designed and would meet the unique needs of different users. We needed to make sure that clients felt like we had done our user research and had a solution, even if it was productized, that met their needs."*

Also, rather than emphasizing how a digital product was less expensive to deliver, Strategy Execution talked about how it helped "democratize learning and improve career mobility and opportunities for employees. The value was less about price and more about being inclusive and equitable with the services that they're providing," shared Ansbro. This messaging reinforced Strategy Execution's market positioning as a premium provider of project management training known for customized, cutting-edge content and learning experiences.

They also worked with partners such as Duke University's Duke Corporate Education and Fuqua Business School to co-brand one of the products and help signal that the product was premium. Ansbro shared,

> *"There was an expensive in-person version of the program developed with Duke, but there was also an online version that could be provided to more people. To be consistent with our market positioning, it was important that there was a premium version of our premium product but that there was also a more scalable version of a premium product."*

There are four primary types of packaging strategies:

1) All-Inclusive: This really is not a packaging strategy because everything is included for one fixed price. There is no differentiation of features by customer segment. This is most common early in a product's maturity when you are still trying to determine which features are most valuable and to whom[21]. If your strategy is to grow a separate products business, this is a difficult packaging structure to keep longer term because there is no way to "land and expand" other than adding users. However, if your product is typically bundled with services, an all-inclusive option might make sense to keep longer term.

2) Feature-Based Packaging: Packages are differentiated based on different features or capabilities.

A common type of feature-based packaging is **good/better/best.** This model, also known as tiered pricing, involves offering several product versions at different price points and feature sets. Each tier caters to different customers' needs and budgets with the "good" package being the most basic and affordable, the "better" offering more features, and the "best" providing premium features at a higher price. The end-user is typically the same, but they may have different priorities, budgets, and primary needs. This can help support a land-and-expand strategy because customers may see the "good" package as a lower risk way to try you out and then expand to more features as they use and trust the product.

Another version of feature-based packaging happens when you have different end users with different urgent and expensive problems. For example, HubSpot provides a suite of tools aimed at different business functions within an organization. Its MarketingHub package focuses on marketing professionals and provides features such as email marketing, content management, SEO tools, and marketing automation. The urgent and expensive problem here is generating leads and converting them into customers. Conversely, its SalesHub package targets sales professionals. Its features include email tracking, meeting scheduling, sales quotes, and a robust CRM system. The urgent and expensive problem is streamlining sales processes and enhancing customer interactions. The overarching organizational problem that HubSpot solves is business growth and customer management, but the packages map to different users and their urgent and expensive problems. This can also support a land-and-expand strategy because you can expand to different functions or end-user types.

3) By Consumption: This is the all-inclusive model where rather than paying one fee to access all features, all customers pay a standard fee for access to a base platform or base set of features and then pay for additional features or services as they use them[22]. This is also well suited for a land-and-expand strategy and typically is not introduced until a product is more mature and you have a good sense of the market's willingness to pay for using additional features.

4) Modular/Create Your Own: In this flexible approach, customers can customize their package by selecting from a range of features or modules to use from day one. This allows for a personalized product experience and caters to specific customer preferences or requirements. Having add-ons to existing packages, like the environmental consulting firm provided, is also a way to provide more flexibility without having a completely modular approach. Add-ons are best when a need does not apply across all customers.

As your product begins to mature, you will likely create more packages. This is because you may be expanding into new market segments or you see a way to segment your target market more finely, and, therefore, more accurately tailor pricing through different packages.

For example, Mercer, a global HR consultant, has, for a long time, offered reports that companies can purchase on a one-off retail basis (i.e., modular/create your own packages). Mercer then introduced the Talent All Access® Platform (TAAP), an all-inclusive subscription to the full portfolio of reports. As the individual products matured, the firm introduced new packages for both different geographies and different user personas (i.e., feature-based packages).

For example, rather than selling one package that included aggregate compensation data for all geographies, which was of most value to multinational companies, it created smaller priced packages for each region and each country so that smaller companies that only operated in one or two geographies could purchase packages that were tailored to their needs. This allowed the product to expand beyond Mercer's core client group of large multinationals and created an option for companies with a smaller geographic footprint.

Packages versus Bundles

When organizations combine products with complementary services or additional items that enhance the primary product's value, we call those bundles rather than product packages. A bundle creates more value for the customer by providing a comprehensive solution that not only meets their basic requirements but also offers additional benefits that are not available when purchasing the product alone.

For example, when the sales training company Miller Heiman created Scout[23], a subscription-based sales analytics platform, it was not sold as a standalone; it was bundled with Miller Heiman's sales skills development or methodology programs. John Riley, the former head of sales of Miller Heiman, shared, "Scout was never sold as a standalone because it was always based on our methodology and skills training. The software was designed to reinforce the application of the sales methodology and reinforce the skills training taught by Miller Heiman."

When done well, this complementary approach can act like rocket fuel for your business and provide a significant competitive advantage. Complementary products can be bundled with services in attractive packages that offer better value or convenience to the customer. Bundling can also encourage the trial of new products and increase the stickiness of your services. Introducing complementary products opens cross-selling opportunities, allowing you to leverage existing relationships and sales channels to promote new offerings and diversify revenue.

Bundles are often priced attractively compared to purchasing each component separately, providing an incentive for customers to choose the bundled offering over individual products or services. Also, the seller typically has flexibility to configure the bundle (but not always, as we'll explore below), and the product and services are typically listed as separate line items so clients can redline them as well as run them through different procurement processes, if needed.

In contrast, product packages segment the core product into different tiers or versions to target diverse customer needs and price sensitivities. The focus is on market segmentation, allowing customers to choose a product version that best fits their specific needs and budget without necessarily enhancing the value of the core product itself.

One common go-to-market strategy for services businesses who are productizing is to bundle their product or productized service with more traditional services. In fact, if it's appropriate for the needs of the market, some organizations may go as far as to mandate that the product be included in every new service proposal. For example, when it first launched Scout, Miller Heiman included twelve months of free access to Scout to all sellers who completed their skills training program. This was to both encourage rapid market adoption and to get more usage and market feedback to inform the product roadmap.

We consider this strategy to be a cousin of product-led growth, a go-to-market strategy where the product drives customer acquisition, conversion, and expansion by offering immediate value, promoting itself through user-driven word of mouth. A notable B2B example is Slack. It starts as a free communication tool that teams gradually embed deeper into their workflows, leading to paid upgrades for more features and integrations.

One big consideration for going to market with the product as a free trial as part of a larger services engagement is you still need dedicated resources to onboard customers, ensure they use the product, and convert them to paid customers after the trial.

As your product matures, the component of the bundle that is productized will likely grow. For example, when the law firm Vorys first launched eControl, a technology-enabled solution that helps companies maintain brand control in online sales, the brand monitoring software, Precision eControl, was bundled with services such as policy creation and policy enforcement. However, they have now built software modules to create policies and to manage distribution, which makes enforcement easier. The new product features have displaced the need for the services. The impact on profitability is significant as Whitney Gibson, managing partner, shared,

> *"We think of the productization journey in terms of profitability. You go from low to medium to high profitability and the services intensity declines over that journey. Soon the customers will just need the set-up services."*

We see the same shift happen in product-native businesses. On average, B2B SaaS companies derive about 36 percent of their revenue from services when they are young and just hitting $5 million in revenue. The services could be from onboarding and setup, training, or custom development work. As they mature, that number shrinks to less than 20 percent of revenue[24].

Whether packaging or bundling, be thoughtful about the unique customer segment needs that each package or bundle addresses. Also, beware of packaging in or bundling in features or products that do not appeal to most of the market. These are referred to as "bundle killers." A classic example would be if McDonald's packaged coffee with a hamburger value meal. Coffee is better as an add-on because most customers won't want it[25].

Price Calculation Model

The price calculation model refers to how the price is calculated. Is it based just on package features or does variable usage also influence the price point? For example, in the environmental consulting example from earlier, all packages are offered on an annual subscription basis with the price adjusted not just by the features in that package (heavy, precision, or sustainable) but also according to plant size and energy consumption.

Products can be bundled by size or quantity, offering customers a choice based on their usage or consumption levels. For example, a software product might have different licensing options based on the number of users (e.g., single-user, five-user, and unlimited-user licenses).

Most importantly, **the price calculation models should tie to the value the customer receives, also known as "units of customer value."** That means that the number of users may not be the best metric. For example, in email marketing solutions, pricing is often based on the number of contacts or number of emails sent[26].

The price calculation model may also include discount tiers that reward higher usage. You see this a lot in data storage, where the per-gigabyte cost decreases as more data is used. Or the cost per user decreases as an organization hits new thresholds of users. Higher use should have economies of scale, justifying the discounts. Volume discounts can also increase customer loyalty, as businesses are incentivized to consolidate their use to benefit from volume discounts.

Early in a product's maturity, we often see a debate between whether pricing should be simple, such as all-enterprise access, or conservative and priced by usage.

In general, we recommend keeping the pricing very simple and inclusive early on. From a product perspective, this allows you to see what features users use, who uses it, and how usage expands. However, make it very clear this is initial charter or beta pricing, so it is easier to migrate customers when you have a better sense of features used and the forecasted growth in usage. Then, you can create more complex feature-gated packages and go from enterprise licenses to seat-based licenses or other usage tiers.

For example, one market research firm initially launched with a $200,000 all-enterprise access price. As the product began to mature, they found that their average ICP had thirty active users, and they switched their pricing structure to a $10,000/user price to capture more revenue.

We believe that simple, easy-to-sell pricing is important when the product is early in its maturity, especially if it's being sold alongside many other services, productized services, and/or products. However, as a product becomes more mature, pricing should become more complex because complexity helps you better tailor pricing to the needs and willingness to pay thresholds of different customer segments.

Price Points

Determining the actual price points for different feature packages and usage tiers will be a very iterative process that will be influenced by the inputs we discussed earlier: product strategy and market positioning, customers' willingness to pay, competitors' pricing, and the product's economics. In other words, this is a very dynamic, complex, and more "art than science" process.

We like to give most companies a few general pieces of advice as they start experimenting with different price points.

First, strongly consider a "step on" price point, especially for subscription-based products where the potential lifetime value of a customer is large if they continue to renew or for productized offerings where you can use the land-and-expand strategy we discussed earlier. This is why the strategy of product-led growth—or offering a trial or freemium version of the product—is so effective, but having initially low price points can be very hard for services-based organizations with traditionally high price tag service engagements. The CEO of one training company described the importance of this strategy as,

> *"Our traditional sales mindset was to secure the largest initial deal out of the gate and care a lot less about the tail, because we did not really have an offering with a tail. We had to change our mindset and focus first on acquiring customers, even if it was at the lowest step-on option and later growing and renewing them."*

As the product matures, we also advise identifying the *least* price-sensitive segment of the market and designing a package for them, if it is aligned with your market positioning (this is harder to do if your market positioning is the low-cost provider). Like the luxury consumer segments in B2C markets, these B2B segments often prioritize factors such as exclusivity, premium quality, advanced features, and high levels of service over cost. This is especially prevalent in industries where the cutting-edge performance or reliability of a product can significantly impact business operations or where compliance and security are critical.

Finally, make sure to price the package or tier for the largest customers appropriately high because they will have the most bargaining power on the product roadmap. Although it is typically not an explicit feature, influence on the product roadmap is a significant benefit for those customers who have the largest amount of spend with you and should not be undervalued.

Pilot, Phase In, and Iterate

Determining the actual price points for different feature packages and usage tiers will be a very iterative process.

In your charter/closed beta phase, you are piloting pricing with a small group of low-risk prospects. You want to have a thoughtful and communicated list price point to anchor them on and then typically a discount that recognizes that the product still has some kinks that are being worked out. The amount of the discount should be determined by the owner of the go-to-market strategy for the product, typically the product "founder," and it is okay to actively experiment with pricing at this stage. But price experimenting, again, should be led by the product founder, who should also be doing most of the sales or team selling with a trusted sales resource.

If the product is incredibly immature and you are doing a free pilot or alpha phase, keep in mind that you only need to offer it for "free" to only a handful of customers, and the free phase should be for a defined period, after which they know up front it converts to discounted beta. There may even be a penalty charge if the alpha client chooses not to continue into the discounted beta phase.

For example, one large HR services firm that we worked with had a very new-to-world product and then had a free six-month alpha pilot with three customers that then converted into a discounted beta of 25 percent off an annual $500,000 licensing fee. All alpha customers continued, but if they hadn't, they would have owed a $50,000 cancellation fee. This not only helped the firm work out the product kinks with invested customers but, because of the large product price tag, gave the pilot customers enough advance warning of how the fees would grow over time: $0 the first six months, $375,000 the next twelve months (25 percent off $500,000), and then $500,000 the following year. One executive observed,

> *"It's very hard to ask a customer for a recurring expense of five to seven hundred thousand dollars in October and get it in January. Our alpha and then discounted beta phases helped us get initial customers in but also worked around their multi-year budgeting cycles. We had to structure the pilots and price changes thinking about our customers' buying process and budgeting cycle."*

As you complete the closed beta and start pitching the product to existing customers and new prospects, pricing and packaging will continue to evolve based on what you are learning from the market.

At this phase, many services organizations find that they need to make pricing adjustments that consider the customer experience when they are buying both services and products.

One challenge we commonly see is when a product appeals to existing customers but is only priced and packaged as if the customer was not also buying services. In other words, there is not an option for a service + product bundle where the pricing makes economic sense for the customer.

For example, one company we worked with provides "expert network" services to broker conversations with industry experts for companies researching an investment decision or to get advice on entering a new market.

After many years in the market with the pay-per service, they introduced a new offering where the company would interview industry experts on behalf of their customers and synthesize the findings into syndicated research reports. Those reports are available via a portal that clients can access on an unlimited basis for one flat annual subscription fee.

Many clients would want to use a mix of reports from the library and expert network services for the same project, but there were no bundled ways to purchase. The chief revenue officer shared,

> *"The client experience was the last thing considered when building the go-to-market plans, including pricing, and we were caught off guard because the product had been built and launched independent of the existing service. The product and delivery teams were completely different; however the sales team was responsible for selling both to the same end customer. Customers would naturally ask, 'What do I get if I buy both?' and we did not have a value proposition for buying both."*

Part of the magic of good go-to-market strategy is thinking through different buying and service scenarios. What will it be like for an existing client? A new client? A client that already has Product A? A client that already has Product B? Eventually, you need value propositions for those different scenarios.

And the best way to uncover this is to iterate and be comfortable changing pricing. In fact, revisiting pricing every six to twelve months is okay. Hopefully, you are continuing to make the product more valuable, which should impact pricing. Standard practice is for multiyear contracts to include 5–10 percent annual price increases[27].

We see fear hold back organizations from changing pricing, especially if they have larger customers on the services side. For example, we often hear internal pushback that they don't want to "nickel and dime" large services customers on product price adjustments.

There are tactics for changing pricing that may make price increases easier, such as grandfathering in early customers and migrating them to new list prices over a period. This speaks to the earlier point about giving customers transparency into how prices are going to change over time. The amount of additional revenue that you can generate by merely migrating early discounted customers to new list prices can be significant. For software-as-a-service products, for example, this can generate somewhere between two to five times more annual recurring revenue (ARR)[28].

You can also keep price points the same but change the amount of usage covered by a price (e.g., 150 users rather than 200 users) or adjust the features included.

Most important is to lead price change communications with the value the product is generating and justify the price changes based on increases in value (e.g., new features). A key question to ask is has the organization truly delivered the value they are charging that new price for? If so, customers should understand they are getting a deal and see a reasonable path to increases. If not, or if they are price takers in a market, it'll be harder. A question that is common to gauge product-market fit (and price elasticity) is "How disappointed would you be if you could no longer use product X?" If under 40 percent would be disappointed, getting customers to pay more will be very difficult[29].

Operationalize Prices into the Sales Process

Pricing does not necessarily have to be simple, but it does have to be easy to sell. This means it must make sense to our salespeople, our customers, and not feel like a confusing black box.

The best tool to use to explain prices to your sellers is to create a pricing sheet. It should include:

Package Information

- Prices for different package tiers
- Units of usage driver (e.g. seats)
- Features included per tier
- Term length and payment options
- Any difference by region, customer size, or industry

Add-On Information

- List of available add-ons or bolt-ons
- Pricing per add-on and units of add-on

Service + Product Bundles (if applicable)

- Most common bundles and who each bundle is most appropriate for
- Process for pricing

Available Discounts and Incentives

- List of discounts and incentives
- Rules on discount approvals required
- Rules on term flexibility and approvals required

With each iteration of pricing and packaging, you should update your pricing sheet.

One practical piece of advice is to coach sellers to NOT use pricing tiers and sheets WITH customers. It makes pricing complex and undermines value. As Matt Dixon and Ted McKenna document in their bestseller, *The JOLT Effect*, these types of tactics intended to give customer comfort can wind up increasing customer indecision and kill a sale.

A quick note about discounting. We recommend creating very clear guidelines for the types of discounts offered and when. These should be tied to very specific levels of volume purchased and/or exchanges of value such as referrals to prospective customers, providing a testimonial video, signing a longer contract term, paying up front, or speaking at a customer event. For example, offer a 5 percent discount for referrals to two prospective customers or a testimonial video or a 20 percent discount for a two-year contract paid up front[30].

Order Form versus Proposal

One of the first things you will need to do when you create a more productized offering is to create the order form or client contract. Products are not sold under a master services agreement/engagement letter/statement of work where the client owns the IP and, if you are doing longer-term development work, is treated as a capital expenditure and amortized on the balance sheet by the client. Rather, products have an order form and contract, where the customer does not own the IP and the customer treats the expense as an operating expense flowing through the income statement. If you are selling a bundled solution, it may include both a master services agreement and a product agreement.

Your finance and/or legal team can create this, but make sure that you bring in the right expertise to develop it. You'll want to make sure that the product customer contract is as short and as flexible as possible so that it is perpetually recurring, and you can change prices and terms and conditions like payment intervals and cancellation periods without having to renegotiate the entire contract. You do that by putting things like prices and product descriptions outside the contract in appendices that are subject to change[31]. For example, we find that early in a product's maturity, customers are under-monetized, and you'll want the flexibility to raise prices as the product matures.

Key Takeaways

1. Common mistakes we see when deciding how to monetize new productized offerings include:

   a. Setting prices by simply adding a markup to forecasted costs and missing the opportunity to align prices to customer value

   b. Not aligning pricing to the product strategy

   c. Not researching or test pricing

   d. Setting the same price for all customers and not using complexity to price discriminate between customer segments that have a different willingness to pay

   e. Setting the price too low and/or not raising prices

2. Organizations cannot determine a pricing model until they articulate how the new products or productized services support and/or change their existing business model and how the products will be distributed.

3. Good product pricing is grounded in the economic value the product creates for the customer, particularly the buyer. This starts with understanding the key factors that drive economic value, such as increased revenue, decreased cost, or risk reduction.

4. Packages should be designed to "price the customer segment" and be packages of value that match both the jobs-to-be-done and the willingness to pay for each customer segment.

5. Done well, packages are also an opportunity for you to demonstrate your organization's unique point of view about how your customers' problem presents in different ways and how you have a nuanced understanding of their needs. Well-

designed packages can tell a powerful story about how your offering is better than a customized service.

6. The price calculation models should tie to the value the customer receives also known as "units of customer value." That means that the number of users may not be the best metric.

7. Pricing models don't necessarily have to be simple (although we'd recommend starting there), but they do have to be easy to sell. Do not use too many variables in the pricing model; focus on the key value driver.

8. When looking at competitor pricing, it's not enough to just know their prices for different packages. You must understand their value proposition including features, benefits, and differentiators as well as tiered pricing, discounts, and additional fees. It's also important to understand their pricing strategy. For example, are they bundling products together or offering discounts? Are they trying to be the low-cost option in the market or the premium provider?

9. When raising prices or changing pricing models, focus on how the product has evolved to create more value.

Additional Resources

✗ Pricing model examples

✗ Sample pricing survey questions

✗ Sample pricing sheets

✗ Dynamic SaaS contract framework

✗ Product value matrix template

(Please download the tools at www.commercializebook.com)

CHAPTER 4
MARKETING

Once you have decided WHO you are selling to and WHAT you will do to monetize your new product or productized service (i.e., pricing and packaging), you need to think about HOW you are going to sell it. This starts with marketing and how you are going to message the product's value, reach your target market segment(s), and generate leads.

The good news is that you should already have the foundational ingredients for all of your marketing decisions: customer validation of the problem(s) you are solving, prioritized target market segments, and compelling pricing and packaging.

Now it is time to develop compelling messaging, communicate those messages using the best marketing channels for each target market, and generate the volume of leads necessary to meet revenue targets.

The number one mistake we see organizations make in this phase is underestimating the marketing efforts required.

It is highly likely you will need to make *different* investments in marketing than you already have, especially if you are targeting a different market than the one that consumes your traditional services.

Even if you are targeting the same market, you will need to do some product marketing, which you may not have the skills to do in-house.

Good product marketing is typically focused on customer niches, articulating their problems, and describing how a product solves those problems. It is very different from the broader brand building and thought leadership marketing that a services firm may do to promote their expertise or build brand awareness. These marketing investments will need to be accounted for when creating your business case for productization or making a go/no-go decision on investing in a new product.

For example, we were working with one HR services firm, who, after successful alpha and beta pilots, was launching, in select markets, a new bundled solution that included consulting services plus data and software. Creating the go-to-market strategy and toolkit was a collaborative effort between the product team, the consulting team, and the global marketing team. It quickly became obvious, however, that the marketing team was woefully under-resourced to support a product launch. They had the budget and expertise to identify conferences to sponsor and whitepapers to write, but they did not have expertise creating product demo videos or generating new-to-firm leads with a customer-problem-first approach.

It's also important to think about marketing before the sales channel because, if the marketing is done well, you may need fewer salespeople than you think. Too many services firms are used to being sales-led, but products are more often market-led, as evidenced by the high percentage of the B2B product buying research is done(approximately 70 percent) before a potential customer decides to talk to a sales professional[32].

Marketing is a vast topic, and many resources are available on how to do it well, so we are going to focus on three areas where we see B2B services organizations get stuck:

- Positioning and developing messaging by segments
- Evolving marketing tactics to generate leads
- Iterating quickly

Positioning and Messaging

The foundation of your messaging is your market positioning, which you have been honing all along. Positioning refers to the process of establishing a brand or product in the market and in the mind of the target audience. It involves defining where your product or service fits within the marketplace and how it compares to competitors. The work you did to define who you are selling to (market segmentation and prioritization) and what you are selling (packaging and pricing) created your market positioning. Specifically, your positioning includes:

- Market Differentiation: How does your product or service differ from others in the market?

- Target Audience: Who is your ideal customer and what are their urgent and expensive problems?

- Competitive Landscape: How can you leverage your strengths against your competitors' weaknesses?

- Value Proposition: What unique value do you provide that makes you the preferred choice for your customers?

For example, a B2B software company might position itself as the leading provider of scalable and secure cloud storage solutions for enterprise-level businesses. This positioning would emphasize its strengths in security and scalability, aimed at large organizations needing reliable data management.

In his book *Crossing the Chasm: Marketing and Selling High-Tech Products to Mainstream Customers*, Geoffrey Moore offers a good template for positioning. He suggests outlining an elevator pitch for a product idea:

For (target customers) who are dissatisfied with (the current market alternative), our product is a (new product category) that provides (key problem-solving capability and benefits. Unlike . . . (insert product alternative), our product . . . (insert key product features).

Again, you should already have the inputs to create this based on the work you did to identify your target segments and develop pricing and packaging.

Messaging follows and refers to how your product is the best choice for a specific market segment. This is when you develop specific narratives and key points that communicate the value and positioning of the product or productized services to the target audience(s). It translates the strategic positioning into clear, compelling, and relatable content that speaks directly to the needs and desires of the audience. The messaging is then turned into copy for use across different channels (website, sales collateral, emails, etc.[33])

It includes:

- Customer pain points: How do your communications address specific urgent and expensive problems faced by your customers?

- Key benefits and features: What specific benefits and features of your product or service are highlighted to align with customer needs?

- Secondary messages: What are the unique needs for each market segment? For buyers versus users?

- Urgency drivers: Why should customers buy this now versus waiting a year?

- Differentiators for the product: What makes our product more effective than existing solutions?

- Communication style: How you articulate your value to resonate with the target audience, including the tone and language used.

- Call to action: What actions do you want your audience to take based on your messaging?

For example, continuing with the B2B software company, its messaging might include specific statements like, "Our cloud storage solutions offer unparalleled data protection and scalability, ensuring that your enterprise operates efficiently and securely, even as your data needs grow." This message supports the company's positioning by highlighting key features and benefits that appeal to large enterprises.

Your messaging brings the positioning to life. It is the tactical execution that communicates the positioning to the market through various channels like marketing materials, website content, and sales pitches.

And just because we have seen it too many times, remember that your messaging must ladder back to the urgent and expensive problems you are solving. Each time you talk about a feature, it needs to include a tie back to how it helps solve a customer problem. One marketing executive at a productized services company shared,

> *"People don't buy because of features, but oftentimes we are just talking about all the stuff that we have versus the overarching message and story that all these features ladder up to. Great messaging starts with 'Here are the problems that you have' and then explains how we help."*

Articulating C-Level Benefits

The most effective messaging focuses on the product of the product's product. Yes, you read that right. The most effective ad campaigns market an item that is two or three steps removed from the actual product.

Imagine that you want to sell perfume or cologne. The product is a fragrant, yellow liquid, but why does anyone want a fragrant, yellow liquid? People enjoy smelling nice, that's why. So, the end goal of the product (or the product's product) is secondary to the perfume itself.

But why does someone want to smell nice? The answer is because they want to feel attractive in the eyes of others, making that state of being the product of the product's product. When thinking about every perfume or cologne ad that's ever been made, the commodity being sold isn't just the perfume; it's the hope that the product will make oneself attractive to others. The end goal is several steps removed from the start line.

I'll offer my own company as a good B2B example. At Vecteris, we conduct research and provide training, tools, and coaching (our product) to help organizations innovate and successfully launch new products (our product's product). The new products help our clients scale and create recurring revenue with a higher margin. So, our product's product's product is a way to scale services and generate recurring, high-margin revenue. Once you've uncovered the essence of a product, messaging needs to be developed to market it.

Ideally, your product's product's product should be the resolution of an issue and/or an outcome that the C-level executives at your customer companies care about[34]. And not just one C-level executive but all of them, plus the CEO and the board. For example, if you sell a solution to improve employee engagement at call centers, a benefit may be lower call center costs, higher customer satisfaction, and lower turnover rates, which lower recruiting costs. It may also help you better compete with new market entrants. The exception to this is if you are using a product-led growth strategy where you market directly to the users of the product and then from their use of it, the C-suite sees the true value. So for product-led growth, if you market to users to make their lives easier on a particular job, then they adopt the product (usually free).

Make It Personal

In your customer research, you also want to explore your buyers' personal objectives and motivations, and part of your messaging should speak to them[35]. You'll want to understand not only their business goals but also their personal goals and speak to things such as:

- Reducing hassle
- Increasing clarity
- Reducing friction between organizational silos
- Helping them navigate a time of extreme uncertainty and risk
- Increasing their confidence in decision-making

For example, at Vecteris, we describe our personal buyer value proposition as giving them the confidence to productize and de-risking career-defining decisions.

Tell Stories

The final component of effective messaging includes using case studies, ideally told as stories. Storytelling is powerful. It's a medium that calls people to action and allows them to connect. Paul Zak, founding director of the Center for Neuroeconomics Studies, wrote a *Harvard Business Review* article a few years ago discussing a study that showed how good storytelling "hacks" the oxytocin system to motivate people to engage in certain behaviors[36].

This oxytocin "hack" can be a powerful tool to message the benefits of our product. Zak's advice, "When you want to motivate, persuade, or be remembered, start with a story of human struggle and eventual triumph. It will capture people's hearts—by first attracting their brains."

Secondary Messages by Segment and Persona

Keep in mind that if you are pursuing more than one segment, you'll need messaging by segment. Typically, this evolves as your product matures and is not something you should have on day one.

In addition to having different value propositions and messaging for different buyer roles, you should also consider different messaging and value propositions by maturity of the customer if less mature customers have different needs from more mature customers.

You can use very targeted messaging to bring in the most attractive prospective customers. Focus on developing the messages that are going to bring in truly good leads. One go-to-market executive at a productized services company described them as "tentpole" messages. He said,

> *"What messages are going to speak to our most attractive customer segments? The ones that will make prospective customers sit up and say, 'Oh, yeah, that's me.' Ideally your most qualified leads self-select in because you are speaking directly to them."*

Positioning and Messaging Watch Outs as You Productize

It is important to recognize that as you productize, your positioning and messaging will shift from emphasizing personalization to emphasizing the benefits of standardization.

For customized B2B services, positioning focuses on the provider's ability to understand unique customer needs and create bespoke solutions. The emphasis is on flexibility, expertise, and personalized service. This approach often targets specific niches or high-value clients who require tailored solutions that standard products cannot provide. The messaging often includes case studies about collaboration, understanding specific industry challenges, and providing unique solutions that precisely fit customer requirements. The tone is more personalized, often directly addressing the customer's potential concerns or aspirations, and the content is more detailed, demonstrating deep industry knowledge and problem-solving capabilities.

For example, a cybersecurity firm specializing in bespoke security solutions for financial institutions might position itself as a partner in creating custom, robust security architectures. Messaging would focus on their deep understanding of financial regulations, personalized service, and long-term client relationships.

Contrast that with the positioning and messaging for more productized services, where you are targeting a wider audience, highlighting a universal problem and how the product provides a ready-made solution. You occupy a unique market position not because you customize for each client but because you have benefits such as being more efficient, easy to use, scalable, and cost-effective. Ideally, the messaging for productized services or products emphasizes clear, quantifiable benefits and outlines specific features and potential ROI, making it straightforward for potential customers to understand what they are buying and how it will benefit them. The communication often uses clear, concise language and includes strong calls to action.

For example, a cybersecurity software company offering out-of-the-box solutions for in-house cybersecurity professionals would position its product as easy to deploy and cost-effective, emphasizing protection against common threats and compliance with standard regulations. Messaging would focus on quick setup, cost efficiency, and scalability.

As customized services organizations introduce more productized offerings to the market, they need to make sure that the messaging supports why the offering is more productized and why it is packaged the way it is.

For example, when the sales training company Challenger developed a subscription-based product, the messaging needed to address when and why an always-on, subscription-based approach was superior to a point-in-time solution. Simon Frewer, former CEO of Challenger, shared,

> *"We developed messaging that discussed how an always-on solution complemented a multiday training intervention by supporting long-term behavior change and serving as an 'insurance' policy that they would get an ROI from the training."*

Another great example of a messaging transition is when a sales intelligence company that we work with was transforming their company from one that manually matched clients with sales intelligence experts to one where clients could self-serve and search, match, and schedule with experts using an online platform. They had to be much crisper on the use cases for the solution rather than saying they would offer any type of intelligence. The former chief commercial officer observed,

> *"Before productizing our value proposition focused on how we offered 'human intelligence to support sales.' It was very much we can help you with any sales question. As we productized, we narrowed that to talk about specific points in the sales pursuit where our solution could be used: current tech stack, pain points, buyers, and buying process. This was a fundamental part of standardizing and scaling our approach."*

Bundled Solutions—A Mix of the Two

As mentioned earlier, many B2B services organizations that productize start by bundling products in with existing services. The product is part of a larger solution sale where you are still being consultative and diagnosing customer needs to configure the bundle (even if just choosing from a few preset configurations).

In this case, you need messaging that goes beyond typical customized services messaging (we really get to know your needs) and typical product messaging (faster, cheaper solution to your problem). The best messaging for bundled solutions focuses on how the philosophy behind the approach is better than others. You have a unique point of view on what the customer's problem really is and the best way to solve the problem.

For example, one large HR services firm initially went to market with their new digital talent development and workforce planning tool as a standalone product. Their messaging focused on how it was faster and cheaper than manual efforts. However, they decided to change their go-to-market approach and begin marketing it to existing services customers. The head of delivery said,

> *"We needed a story arc above the standalone product benefits story arc. We landed on 'If you understand your talent, you'll make better investment decisions and you'll retain your best performers.' The messaging fits nicely with the goal of our services to help clients determine the best talent development and acquisition strategies. The messaging needs to drive demand for both the services and the product."*

Marketing Tactics/Lead Generation

Once you have your messaging, you need to communicate those messages using different marketing channels and generate the volume of leads necessary to meet revenue targets.

Diving into the implementation of specific marketing tactics and channels is beyond the scope of this book, and many resources are out there such as *Hacking Growth* by Sean Ellis. But we do want to cover the nuances that are specific to firms that are productizing.

And the biggest one is **you likely don't have the marketing engine you need to generate product leads.**

Data confirms this. Professional services firms have one of the highest lead conversion rates across industries, averaging around 9.2 percent. This means that for every hundred leads a B2B professional services firm generates, around nine of those leads convert into paying customers on average. Compare that to the average B2B SaaS company, which has between a 1 to 2 percent conversion rate[37].

This indicates how much an organization needs to spend on marketing. B2B SaaS companies, for example, have a median marketing spend of 10 percent of revenue, while B2B services companies spend an average of 6.9 percent of their revenue on marketing[38].

Even if you are going to bundle products in with existing services, you may still need incremental marketing spend and different marketing tactics. **The right amount of marketing investment depends on strategy and maturity as well as positioning and price.**

Before discussing matching marketing tactics to your productization strategy and maturity, let's recap the different ways to visualize how a prospective customer becomes a paying customer and the marketing, sales, and customer success activities needed to be successful.

The traditional sales funnel concept is a model that describes the marketing and sales stages prospective customers travel through, from their initial awareness of a product or service to their purchase decision. It's visualized as a funnel because it starts broad at the top with many prospects and narrows down through various stages to the point of purchase, where fewer individuals complete the journey.

As professional services firms introduce products that have recurring revenue such as any subscription-based "as-a-service" product, the traditional framework of a sales funnel needs to be expanded. For example, some people refer to a flywheel of product to marketing, to sales, to customer success as a circular motion with operating processes at the center. Another popular framework is the "bowtie" analogy, which extends the traditional sales funnel concept. Unlike the classic funnel, which narrows down from lead generation to closing a sale, the bowtie analogy acknowledges the importance of post-sale engagement, customer success, and expansion after the point of sale.

Regardless of which visualization you use, you will likely need some marketing efforts to generate and help convert leads. This includes:

- Making your target market segment aware of you and your offerings

- Nurturing leads as they consider whether or not to purchase

This is an oversimplification (again, there are many marketing books and resources available on this), but at different stages of the funnel you will utilize different tactics. And at different stages of product maturity, you will utilize different tactics. Finally, the price point of your product and your productization strategy will also influence which marketing tactics you use.

In other words, **there is no one right marketing tactic formula for going to market with your new product or productized service.**

For example, higher price-point products and productized services (above $100K) will likely rely on a mix of cold calling, in-person events, PR, ads, and even direct mail to initially generate leads and opportunities. Lower price-point products and productized services will use less expensive tactics such as cold emails, pay per click, content marketing, SEO, affiliate marketing, and partnerships[39].

If your target markets range in price sensitivity, you may also have two completely different funnels/flywheels/bowties—one for lower priced segments and one for premium segments.

You should also be using lower-cost marketing tactics for brand-new products for which you are still honing your product-market fit. After you validate product-market fit, you will graduate to using more of a "growth marketing" approach (more on that later), where you are rapidly testing tactics to figure out what works.

Also, some of these, such as SEO, are slower to take hold, so they are most effective when a product is more mature. Conversely, some are not very scalable, such as in-person events, so they are best used when the product is less mature.

Finally, different tactics will be used at different phases of the customer journey. For example, marketing tactics will be different at the building awareness phase (e.g., PR, conferences, advertising) than when awareness has been achieved and differentiating our product from the competition is the goal (through webinars, nurture campaigns, etc.).

Keep in mind that marketing channels are rapidly evolving. For example, analysts forecast that traditional search engine volume could drop by as much as 25 percent in just the next one to two years with search marketing losing market share to AI chatbots and other virtual agents[40].

Selling to New or Existing Customers and Target Markets

Another big factor that could dramatically change the marketing resources needed is whether the product or productized service will be sold to your current customers or new customers. If you are selling to new customers, lead generation resources will be needed and at a scale higher than you may have had to bring in new services clients because, as you saw in the benchmarks, conversion rates and contract value is typically lower. That means you'll need more leads if you want your product revenue to match or surpass your services revenue.

If your market is new customers, then you may also be marketing to new market segments where you have less expertise in reaching them and little brand recognition. Most buyers of B2B products are doing a significant amount of research before talking to a salesperson, which means you'll need marketing efforts to ensure that your products or solutions are found.

Three Favorite Tactics

We do have a few favorite marketing tactics for organizations that are productizing: content marketing, integration marketing, marketplaces.

We are big fans of **content marketing** (blogs, surveys, webinars, videos, whitepapers), especially for bundled solutions where the solution may be more complex than a simple product or services sale. The best messaging for bundled solutions focuses on how the philosophy behind the approach is better than others. You have a unique point of view on what the customer's problem really is and the best way to solve the problem. That is worthy of content. It also is valuable given the data that more and more B2B buyers want to do their own research before talking to sales and that "content interest" is one of the most effective predictors of intent[41].

Once the content is created, we suggest using the "rolling thunder" approach outlined in the book *Product Launches* by Mary Sheehan. Although the book is written on how to launch products at more mature tech-native, product-native companies, this approach refers to creating marketing assets once and repackaging them to use over and over. For example, creating a whitepaper and then using parts of it in blogs, social content, and emails. The same can be done with content from events, longer videos, etc.[42].

At a lot of professional services firms, content marketing is distributed to partners or other professionals who write articles, whitepapers, LinkedIn posts, and other forms of thought leadership. If they are only writing about custom services, it will make it harder to shift the brand perception in the market.

Additionally, thought leadership should be supporting your unique point of view that differentiates your solutions and tools, not just your expertise. For example, a vice president of product at one large services firm shared,

> *"Product marketing is still nascent here. We have a well-known brand and most of our marketing is thought leadership created by our consultants when they have a gap between projects. But that thought leadership is designed to showcase the expertise of the person writing it. It rarely highlights the problems that our new products and tools have been designed to solve. We are not doing much problem-solution fit marketing that we need to tout our products."*

If your product or productized service can integrate with another product or service, another effective tactic could be **integration marketing.** This is where you integrate with a partner and you both promote the integration[43]. A classic example of this is HubSpot and Shopify, integrating HubSpot's marketing automation and Shopify's ecommerce platform. They jointly market the integration through various channels. This includes co-authored blog posts, joint webinars, and shared success stories.

For example, Finit is the leading implementation partner for OneStream Software, an enterprise corporate performance management software platform. When OneStream announced that they were going to launch a Solution Exchange with a portion of the exchange dedicated to partner-developed solutions, Finit jumped at the chance and launched three solutions on the new partner marketplace. The solutions create stickiness with their existing clients beyond the initial implementation phase, but they have also provided a new channel for all OneStream customers to find and engage with Finit. Since launching the solutions on the OneStream PartnerPlace, Finit has added new recurring revenue subscriptions to supplement their legacy time and materials business.

This is also an example of leveraging an existing **marketplace** where your target buyers are actively present and looking, such as the AWS marketplace, which allows independent software vendors and data providers to market and sell their solutions directly to AWS customers. Other well-known ones include Microsoft AppSource and Azure Marketplace, Google Cloud Marketplace, Salesforce AppExchange, Red Hat Marketplace, etc. Effectively marketing and selling on each of these marketplaces is a specialized skill, so we suggest finding a vendor who has strong experience in them and find a way to quickly test their effectiveness. This is also where marketing strategy becomes a sales channel decision[44], as we'll discuss in the next chapter.

Importance of a Website

If your strategy is to sell products alongside or instead of your services and you already have a strong brand in the market, it's important that corporate marketing helps support shifting how the brand is perceived in the market. You will need to tout what is new. And the best place to start is your website.

Again, how to design a good website is not in the scope of this book, but the website for a product company will be different from a customized services company. For example, to build trust and credibility with potential clients, most professional services firms' websites emphasize their expertise and experience by showcasing the firm's experts, their credentials, and the depth of experience the team has in providing professional services[45].

In contrast, website messaging for a product or a productized service needs to immediately indicate:

- Target customer segment(s)

- Urgent and expensive problem (s) it solves

- Benefit it provides

- Different use cases

- Cost (if you are ready to publish it)

- Testimonials/logos—reasons to believe

- High level how will I use it

- How to get started[46]

If, for example, part of your company's brand promise, as featured on the website, is that you take a very customized approach with each customer, that component will be incongruent with the brand of a more scalable product. "You can't keep your old website that just talks about all your consulting services. It confuses customers right off the bat," says Dejan Duzevik. When he was chief product officer at Concentric, an analytics software firm that began as a consulting firm, Dejan says one of the biggest mistakes they made was waiting until after they had launched products to think about their brand. He said that in his ten years at Concentric, the greatest impact on revenue occurred when they refreshed the company brand to match their new product strategy.

Another chief product officer whose firm completely sunset customized services for a more productized services approach shared, "You need a website that clearly defines who you are. It was incredibly hard for us to sell a new productized approach when our website did not show us as productized."

Keep in mind that irrespective of contract value, most B2B buyers will do their learning using your website. For example, Gartner expects

80 percent of B2B sales interactions between suppliers and buyers to occur digitally. This B2B buying shift toward a digital—first model has accelerated over the past couple of years. In fact, 33 percent of *all* buyers report preferring a seller-free sales experience, with 44 percent of *millennial* B2B buyers saying they prefer a seller-free sales experience [47].

Your website is also critically important if you are going to need any e-commerce, free-trial, or freemium version capabilities, as we'll discuss later.

Agile Marketing

We were working with an organization who was developing their first product, and they were lucky enough to have a head of marketing. We were brought in to help define the product requirements based on market needs, not develop the go-to-market plan. The head of marketing created a marketing plan for product launch that extended out for eighteen months. It included a lot of things you would expect but left no room for learning and changing tactics. This is especially important when you are new to productization.

For organizations that are new (or newish) to productization, we are big fans of "agile marketing." Like agile software development, the goal of agile marketing is to get marketing ideas into the market quickly to learn from the market's reactions and use those reactions to inform future phases of work. Andrea Fryear, CEO of Agile Sherpas, a firm that helps companies adopt agile marketing methods, describes agile marketing as follows:

> *"Agile marketing is a smaller and more iterative means of communicating with an audience. It is very different from the more traditional approach of spending nine months creating the perfect campaign. When you're going to market with something new, or you're marketing to a new segment, or you're trying to*

change your brand messaging, you can still do a large multi-month or even multi-year plan, but you keep everything but the next step flexible. You test a little bit of copy, design, and tactics, analyze the results, then refine and test a little bit more copy, design, and tactics."

Another somewhat similar marketing philosophy that uses a lot of iteration is "growth hacking," a term coined by Sean Ellis, who played key roles in the growth phases of several successful companies, including Dropbox and Eventbrite. It refers to high-speed and experimental methods for finding, reaching, and learning from customers to hone your go-to-market strategy and marketing tactics after you have validated product-market fit. It's a continuous process, like lean start-up/lean product methods where you quickly ideate, prioritize, test, and analyze different marketing tactics[48]. Like agile marketing, growth hacking eschews traditional marketing plans, pricey launches, and big ad spend.

The Importance of Measures and Assumptions when Experimenting

Again, to do this well, you'll have to have decided on measures of success and make assumptions on how successful different marketing approaches will be. Common outcome measures are things like leads, marketing qualified leads, and customer acquisition costs. Leading indicators and channel metrics will also be important especially once you can prove their relationship with outcomes. These include measures such as website traffic, downloads, reshares, press mentions, conversion rate increase, demo requests, open rates, etc. Until you have established a baseline, you can use benchmarks to forecast performance (e.g., a 25 percent email open rate and 2 percent email conversion rate is fantastic.[49])

As you mature, you'll eventually be able to create a new "revenue operating model," which is a fancy term for the performance measures and goals that you need to achieve at each stage of the marketing, sales and, for subscription products, customer success cycle[50]. **You already have one revenue operating model for customized services. You're effectively adding another one and will need to build a second revenue operating model for your productized services or products and determine the investment in marketing and sales (and approach) that makes sense given the product economics such as average deal size.** It includes assumptions for measures such as the average deal size, cycle time, win rates, and conversion rates at each stage. It's called a revenue operating model because, based on your revenue target, you can calculate the number you need at each funnel stage to get to revenue goals.

Keep in mind that you may need different performance goals for different segments that move faster or slower or that have different conversion rates. Services-only, bundled solutions, and products will also have completely different assumptions as illustrated at the beginning of this chapter when we talked about the 9 percent conversion rate of leads in professional services versus the 1 to 2 percent conversion rate of leads in software products.

Even after you have validated go-to-market fit and determined the best marketing tactics to reach your target market segments, as your value proposition evolves, as you expand to new customer segments, and as competitors evolve their products and customer acquisition tactics, you will also need to continue to evolve your go-to-market approach.

Subscription products offer another example of how your learning will necessitate evolving your marketing approach. As a subscription product begins to mature, you gain a better understanding of the types of customers that are more likely to renew. As this happens, you should evolve your lead qualification criteria because you want leads that don't just buy but also will renew[51]. This is just another reminder to understand what motivates and drives buyers of productized offerings (versus customized services) and shape marketing strategies accordingly.

Marketing Functions

In the first chapter, we discussed how early in a product's maturity your go-to-market strategy and the early execution should be owned by a strong product leader who has stronger-than-average commercial skills. Your positioning likely is not well developed enough until you have closed ten to thirty deals (depends on deal size), so do not hand this off to marketing until then. Similarly, don't make the mistake of developing the go-to-market strategy without the help of existing marketing and sales functions. Leverage marketing and sales, but positioning needs to be owned by the product leader. As you mature, the product leader will transition to doing more of what's called marketing enablement—key messages, content strategy, and perhaps some content creation.

Product Marketing

Product marketing develops the marketing strategy for the product, including (but not limited to) customer targeting, content, feature naming, and messaging by segment. It also supports market research, including voice of the customer and competitive research, and if a technical product, may manage relationships with technology analysts at organizations such as Gartner or Forrester. When launching a new product, marketing needs to be tightly aligned with product management. In less mature organizations, and for brand-new products, this role is assumed by the product leader.

This is separate from corporate marketing that is focused on the organization's brand awareness. It is also separate from any centralized efforts for demand generation (creating and executing campaigns, qualifying leads, cold outreach, etc.).

Again, if you are new to productization, it may be years until you decide to invest in dedicated product marketing. But even when you do, you still need product leaders who understand marketing. One CEO shared, "A good product leader will incorporate marketing early in the product development process and see the value in marketing."

As you move out of the stage of validating product-market fit and into validating go-to-market fit, you'll need more cross-functional, generalist marketing skill sets to experiment effectively.

Growth Marketing

Growth marketing is another function or role you may consider to accomplish your "growth hacking." This role is focused on figuring out the best channels to use to reach prospective customers, typically focused on lower cost channels such as digital ads, social media, SEO, content marketing, webinars, and email campaigns. It focuses on testing a lot of different approaches, for example, A/B testing landing pages, email campaigns, retargeting, and more to refine what works best in engaging and converting users.

Think of product marketing as focusing on the product positioning and messaging and growth marketing focused on the different channels to attract and guide customers through the funnel.

Again, you typically do not invest a lot in trying different channels and scaling your marketing through different channels until you have the messaging well honed, which is why more mature organizations will hire product marketing before growth marketing. If, however, your product leader is playing the product marketing role, then after you have validated the messaging, you may want to invest in growth marketing to scale. One experienced marketing leader observed,

"Growth marketers take the messaging from the product leader or product marketer and disseminate it out into the world. Then the growth marketer can let you know how the messaging is performing by segment and channel. Product marketing is strategy and growth marketing is channel execution."

A Word About Product-Led Growth

As mentioned in the previous chapter when talking about allowing users to get value from the product before paying for a certain period, product-led growth can be an effective go-to-market strategy. As a reminder, a free trial or "freemium" use of the product and then realizing value from product use is what drives customer acquisition, conversion, and expansion, not a salesperson. Think Spotify, Canva, or Slack.

Some organizations have decided to increase the cost of the services, so it appears that the product part of the bundle is free. This typically works well when the product is new and usage may not be immediate but will increase in value as the services engagement proceeds/later in the services engagement.

The advantage of this approach is that it typically leads to shorter sales cycles, lower customer acquisition costs (it can help when sales/marketing budgets are constrained), and higher customer lifetime values because they have tried the product before committing to buy and are less likely to churn and have already qualified themselves. Product-led growth also plays into buyers' desire to self-educate and not talk to a salesperson until they are ready to buy.

There are many resources on how to do product-led growth well (such as *Product-Led Growth* by Wes Bush or Elena Verna's *Growth Scoop* newsletter[52]). However, they are geared toward tech-native, product-native firms. Because we see a lot of services firms who have a strategy of selling their products bundled in with services and may want to launch by offering the product as a free part of the bundle, like Miller Heimen did with Scout, it's important that you know the keys to making this flavor of product-led growth successful at a high-level.

Product-led growth is not for every product, as more complex, higher contract value products benefit from a sales-led approach. It can also be hard to implement product-led growth, as you need to ensure that free users are still well onboarded and nurtured to eventually convert into paid customers. If you do not have many competitors and/or are in a new product category and you need to create demand with a lot of customer education, product-led growth is not a great strategy[53].

If you decide to use product-led-growth, you'll need to decide between using a freemium or a free trial approach. Freemium works well when you have a large market and you are positioning yourself as a low-cost provider, because it keeps your costs low, assuming the product is easy to self-serve[54]. Slack, Zoom, and HubSpot are all great examples. With this model, you are often marketing the freemium version directly to users who then become internal champions who persuade IT buyers to purchase the product for company-wide use[55].

If you are targeting an underserved niche and have more of a premium (e.g., higher price) market positioning, a free trial or traditional sales channel with a demo approach is better[56].

In other words, free trials can be a good marketing tactic for low-dollar, high-volume, high-velocity use cases. If you are using a free-trial approach, however, you'll need to ensure that the "time to value" is aligned with the period of the free trial. For example, the chief marketing officer of a software integration firm who has been experimenting with offering a thirty-day free trial shared,

"What I'm finding is that our free 30-day trial, which provides full access, isn't converting. And it's not converting because full access is overwhelming and has many different use cases.

So now I'm experimenting with offering a 30-day trial that is just for one use case around connecting NetSuite to Shopify. Focusing on one specific integration may narrow the initial customer base that signs up for the free trial, but if they are successful during the trial period, they should be more likely to convert to paid."

And, it should go without saying, the value delivered during the free trial should match the perceived value. If users cannot easily use the product in the time allotted or if you have miscommunicated or misunderstood the value customers receive, then your product-led growth strategy will fail[57].

Another alternative approach is a sales-led workshop trial where a specific situation is created for the customer to solve a problem using the product. The parties agree up front on criteria for the trial, and the buyer will move forward in the sales process if minimum criteria are met. These could be technical, strategic, ease of use, or other types of criteria.

Paid trials are also a valuable alternative to explore above product-led growth. For a set time—say three months—the buyer will consume both services and the product, evaluating performance against criteria like those listed above. A best practice is to write opt-in or opt-out clauses into the trial agreement so that the buyer can move forward with full contracting immediately upon satisfying decision criteria in the paid trial. This approach works well because it creates the business case for the buyer and seller using the buyer's specific use case and employees.

You'll also need to be clear on what usage measures signal that the users are getting value from the product so you can nurture them/stimulate usage. And there needs to be an owner to champion the use of the product while it is in a trial period. This could be part of the customer success function or the product leader if the product is less mature. We strongly recommend that you do *not* make it the responsibility of the delivery team. Their incentives and, more importantly, their professional DNA, is rarely wired to promote product use.

Key Takeaways

1. You will need to make *different* investments in marketing than you already have, especially if you are targeting a different market than the one that consumes your traditional services. Even if you are targeting the same market, you will need product marketing capabilities, which you likely do not have in-house. These marketing investments will need to be accounted for when creating your business case for productization or making a go/no-go decision on investing in a new product.

2. Your messaging must ladder back to the problems you are solving. It is *not* about the features. If you talk about a feature, it needs to include a tie back to how it helps solve a customer problem.

3. As you productize, your positioning and messaging will shift away from emphasizing personalization to emphasizing the benefits of standardization.

4. If you are bundling products in with existing services, you need messaging that goes beyond typical customized services messaging (we really get to know your needs) and typical product messaging (faster, cheaper solution to your problem). The best messaging for bundled solutions focuses on how the philosophy behind the bundled solution approach is better than others. There is a unique point of view on what the customer's problem really is and the best way to solve the problem.

5. You likely don't have the marketing engine you need to generate product leads. Professional services firms have one of the highest lead conversion rates across industries, averaging around 9.2 percent versus a B2B SaaS company, which has between a 1 to 2 percent conversion rate.

6. There is no one right marketing tactic formula for going to market with your new product or productized service. The right amount of marketing investment and the right tactics depends on strategy and maturity as well as positioning and price.

7. Do not create long-term marketing plans or invest in permanent product marketing or growth marketing capabilities before truly validating product-market fit and growth tactics.

8. As you mature, you'll be able to create a new revenue operating model for the performance measures and goals that you need to achieve at each stage of the marketing, sales and, for subscription products, customer success cycle. You already have one revenue operating model—for customized services— but you will need to build a second revenue operating model for your productized services or products and determine the appropriate investment in marketing and sales that you'll need to hit revenue goals.

Additional Resources

✕ Positioning statement (a.k.a. "elevator pitch") template

✕ Product benefits identification worksheet

✕ Multi-channel marketing campaign planning template

(Please download the tools at www.commercializebook.com)

CHAPTER 5

CHOOSING YOUR SALES CHANNEL(S)

Remember the story of TalentTether*? To diversify revenue, they built products to complement their traditional outplacement and executive coaching products such as training products designed to reskill existing employees.

They had great positioning and messaging, but the new products were not selling.

Why?

They had not made any adjustments to their sales channel. They put lower cost, lower converting training products into the same sales channel that was selling their traditional higher cost and often bespoke outplacement and executive coaching services.

A former executive described it well when she reflected,

> *"There was limited understanding of the different sales motions and skills that would be required to sell these new products. Not only were the products lower cost, but they were also less urgent*

---

* Pseudonym

than our legacy outplacement services. Our legacy services helped our clients with an urgent need, like heart surgery. The patient is selecting a surgeon, not whether they will have surgery. But the new reskilling products were like helping back pain. I can live with back pain. We had a whole sales team that was used to working with a motivated buyer who had a clear timeline. The new products needed sellers who could generate demand and convince buyers the product was worth their investment of moving beyond the status quo."

In other words, they needed a different sales skill set.

Selling a customized service and selling a more standardized product are two very different things. The divide between selling a custom solution and selling a scalable product is large. The head of product for a global consulting firm put it this way:

"Going to market and selling are hard, and companies should organize around it earlier. We assumed the consultants and partners would be able to sell our new product because they sell a ton of consulting business and are talking to the right people. But the skills for selling consulting services do not automatically transfer into skills for selling standardized products."

Organizations often need a different sales team or channel to sell products. For example, the economics of a product sale are different (typically lower price point but higher margin and higher lifetime value) and rely heavily on lead generation and value-based selling techniques, like demonstrating how a prospect would solve their challenges with a productized offering. Your consultants and partners may not have experience using these sales techniques.

When selling customized services, your sellers—whether they are doer-sellers or dedicated sellers—are using either a consultative selling approach where they act as trusted advisors, helping clients solve complex and unique business problems, or they use a solution selling approach where they focus on identifying specific customer pain points and tailoring solutions to meet those needs, which is crucial in selling customized services.

As you move into selling more productized offerings, you may need sellers who are more skilled in value-based selling approaches like the Challenger sales approach (pushing customers to think differently about their needs and how more standardized approaches can work). **Successfully selling your new products or productized services is not as simple as winning the hearts and minds of your existing sellers.** The truth is that selling productized offerings is an opportunity to create new sales roles and sell through new channels. Starting from your existing structure can often lead to a stall.

Again, there are many resources on how to effectively sell products, from the 1995 classic *Solution Selling* by Michael Bosworth to the recent bestseller *Jolt Effect* by Matt Dixon and Ted McKenna. We want to focus on how to evolve your sales channel(s) when productizing as well as the sales channel considerations when you are introducing products or productized services alongside existing services or as part of a bundled solution that includes both services and products.

Sales Channel Decisions Should Be Guided by Productization Strategy and Maturity

In the early stages of maturity (stage zero, pre-revenue alpha testing), sales is the job of the product leader. The product lead is still acting like a mini general manager or "founder" for the business opportunity represented by the product.

As you move into validating product-market fit, you may allow a small part of your existing sales team to begin to sell the product with the help of the product leader. We call this sales team the "pilot team," although it does not need to be a team. In our experience, most organizations just need a single dedicated seller to get to product-market fit. Once you validate product-market fit, many different sales channel options are available to you, which we'll discuss below. For example, you could decide at that point to invest in a dedicated product sales team, roll out to your existing services sellers, or even use a channel partner. Or, depending on your strategy, you may use a hybrid model.

Let's explore all the options.

Pilot Team

Again, the first deals to validate product-market fit should be brought in by the product leader. (The actual number of deals will vary, depending on the average deal size.) That is because you'll need to validate the assumptions in your initial launch plan.

- Do you have the right ICP?

- Is your pricing appropriate? Your packaging?

- Is the customer buyer journey really what you initially mapped out?

- What are the best ways to generate leads?

- How effective are the different sales channels?

- What investments do you need to make to improve sales effectiveness?

As you validate product-market fit and move into the next phase of validating go-to-market fit where you create your sales playbook (i.e., sales method, what you say, tools you use, etc.), it can be very helpful to have a pilot team that includes the product leader and a small number of trusted sellers. This is before hiring a dedicated sales force or investing in training the broader existing sales channels.

The sales professionals should be high performers, which means you will have to make it worth their while to take on the risk to their earning potential. Also, how are you going to structure activities so that there is a good feedback loop between them and the product leader?

When Challenger went into its beta phase with its subscription platform, it did not release to its entire sales team. Simon Frewer, former CEO of Challenger, shared,

> *"We put it in the trusted hands of folks that were more flexible, that weren't as rigid. And then we found a few specific opportunities where it made sense to try selling the new platform. A small team of people from product, sales leadership, and a sales professional, iteratively worked to refine the positioning, messaging, packaging, and pricing as we worked through those first opportunities. We learned a lot and changed the pitch a lot before we released it to everybody."*

In our experience, the early sellers should be people who have strong business acumen and are good at spotting market segment needs but don't exaggerate opportunity. Allen Mueller, former CEO at Emissary, observed,

> *"The best salespeople to launch a new product are very measured. They say things like 'I've talked to ten prospects and seven out of ten said this was a problem. And this is what they would spend to solve that problem.' And they are great at spotting new product market opportunities, especially adjacencies. You need a team that is collectively strong at listening and then translating that into a market problem."*

This group should also be tasked with determining whether to leverage your existing sales channels as you scale or if you'll need to invest in new sales channels such as a channel partner.

Existing Sales Team Rollout

Once they validate product-market fit, many organizations decide to sell through their existing channels, which, depending on the organization, could be an army of doer-sellers, a dedicated existing sales team, or a hybrid of the two. This approach may make sense if your strategy is to sell to existing customers and target markets and/ or if your strategy is to sell the more productized service bundled with services.

But as previously noted, many organizations wrongly assume that their existing doer-sellers or even dedicated sales teams will be able to sell the new product because the skills for selling more traditional services do not automatically transfer into skills for selling standardized products. The problem is more acute when you are trying to sell a more productized approach through a doer-seller channel than a dedicated existing services sales team. This is because doer-sellers are used to selling themselves, not something else. Simon Frewer, former CEO of Challenger, put it this way:

> *"When we launched our annual subscription product, we quickly realized that it wouldn't work to sell through our doer-sellers. It requires a different skill set, and we also needed people who were wired to sell something that wasn't perfect yet because we needed to go fast and test and learn."*

Doer-sellers who have used the product themselves tend to be more successful selling it. Many products that we help organizations bring to market started as internal tools that their professionals used to deliver services to scale more. Samantha Polovina, partner and global product category leader over Mercer's Talent All Access Portal (TAAP) product, shared,

> *"We give all of its internal consultants and client facing colleagues access to TAAP, which not only helps them to do their jobs, but also helps them translate the product's value to clients and explain how it can help them."*

You may also struggle to devise a compensation structure that encourages existing sellers to sell lower-priced products. For example, you may struggle with your existing sellers wanting to give the product away for free as a sweetener to land a larger services engagement. This may be a smart strategy if you have a product-led growth approach and a plan to convert free product users into paid users. This may also make sense if your product truly is meant to be a loss-leader for your services. But, oftentimes, we find that neither is true, and your existing team devalues the product, and it never takes off.

Or you may find that your existing sales channels can sell the more productized approach, but growth stalls when you want to expand selling beyond existing services to clients or clients who will buy as part of a bundle. One product leader at a large global services firm observed,

> *"We are only talking to a fraction of the potential market because we do not have a dedicated sales team. I'm convinced*

that if we were our own small business that operated outside of our company, we would have much more growth. But instead, we're just churning away smaller growth, which is just the nature of being a small product at a large consulting firm."

Two questions we often receive are, how do you know when you are ready to move from selling through your existing sales team and build a dedicated team, and when is a good time to rely less on sales as a bundled solution?

Although the timing varies, when more of the bundled solution's value comes from the more scalable content, tech, and/or data products than from the less scalable customized services, that typically is a good time to reduce your reliance on doer-sellers and start to expect more of the solutions revenue to come from a salesforce experienced in product sales.

New Product Sales Team

At some point, especially if your strategy is to sell your products to non-services customers, you may decide to invest in a dedicated product or productized service sales team[58]. Keep in mind that asking your existing services salespeople to drive sales for something a more productized offering can be challenging. While upskilling, retraining, and providing incentives can help, selling products requires different skills and a focus on different outcomes than selling services.

Another reason is because you are getting product-only inbound leads. For example, a large global consulting firm invests in dedicated product sellers when they start receiving inbound leads for the products. Their vice president of product shared,

"If a big consumer goods company calls up and says, 'I was at the European conference, saw your presentation on this topic

and they mentioned your product and I want to learn more,'
that indicates we should start marketing directly."

Products that solve a very discrete pain point are also good candidates to be sold standalone, even if they complement services. For example, the OneStream PartnerPlace solutions developed by Finit can be sold to both existing Finit services customers as well as to companies who did not use Finit for their OneStream implementation thereby reaching customers through a net new channel that didn't previously exist.

Depending on the size of your organization and the growth rate of your product, you may want to start with a fractional and/or contract approach to building your sales team, including fractional revenue operations, if you do not already have a well-functioning lead generation engine for your new product or productized service. Hiring a contract or fractional sales lead can also reduce your risk if you have never hired a product sales team before and have a higher risk of a mis-hire because of your own lack of experience[59]. This approach used by many start-ups can be a low-risk way to ensure you have the lead generation engine and the sales playbook created before hiring account executives, and the fractional and/or contract leader can also make sure you hire the right profile when you are ready to hire individual sellers.

Early sellers should not only have experience selling products or productized services that have similar economics to yours but also be flexible and able to evolve their approach as you continue to learn more about how to scale your go-to-market approach[60].

One big watch-out is to keep in mind that if you are selling a renewable product, the bulk of your revenue will eventually come from renewals, not from new sales, so make sure not to overinvest in the size of this team. Rather, focus investment on customer success, as we will discuss in chapter 6.

If you are planning on selling your products or productized services to complement services, you will need to make sure that your products sales team is well-integrated with your doer-sellers or your dedicated services sellers. Like the conflict issues that you have with an outside channel partner, you will also run into channel conflicts with your own sales teams. For example,

- Who will own the relationship? Who is responsible for each part of the sales process?

- How will commissions be calculated if a doer-seller hands off an opportunity for a product sale?

- What is the escalation path for addressing and resolving conflicts?

- How does the relationship owner change as a client decreases their services revenue and consumes more product?

We also recommend implementing (and using!) a CRM system or lead management tool that tracks lead status, ownership, and interaction to create transparency and prevent disputes over lead ownership. Finally, we recommend shared goals and compensation structures that reward collaboration between channels.

As your productization strategy gains traction, your dedicated product sellers will grow to having a portfolio of products or productized services that they sell. You'll need to think through how to ensure that the most strategically important products get mindshare and whether you will still launch new products with a pilot team approach.

Some organizations we have worked with decide to build a dedicated product sales team and sell products as a standalone before they later bundle them with existing services. This typically happens when the organization is trying to quickly accelerate the productization strategy and does not want the legacy services organization to slow it down or, worse, sabotage it. However, if they decide they want to sell products with legacy services, they often find that the reverse is true—product sales teams struggle to sell services or bundled solutions.

For example, one global consulting firm we worked with took this approach as they sought to quickly develop a digital product line of business. They undertook an abrupt and widespread hiring campaign that brought in many new sales employees from a digitally mature competitor. They were able to quickly get the product into market after buying the talent and capability, but the firm is now struggling to integrate the new digital products into their services lines of business because the new talent does not have relationships with the services leaders or a deep enough understanding of the services business. One firm leader shared,

> *"We have a very good digital product, but the product sales team does not understand our larger business. They don't have relationships with existing clients or even the internal relationships to solution sell, which is a much larger opportunity."*

Sales Engineers

Whether you are standing up a product sales team or selling through your legacy services channel, we strongly recommend investing in sales engineers or a solutions specialist (or their equivalent), especially if they are selling products through their existing sales channel.

Prevedere, the economic forecasting firm, made the decision to invest in a team of sales engineers when they launched their new economic forecasting software that is sold as part of a bundle with their more traditional economic model building services. The team is made up of former consultants who are economists who used the software internally to deliver client work in the past. Rich Wagner, chief executive officer, shared,

> *"Our sales support team has some of our most experienced veterans. They know econometric modeling and they know how to present insights to executives. They do the demos of the software application and educate customers on our methodology, and they help scope the services part of the solution. They know the type of data we will need, how many upfront models we will need to build and the best timeline for implementation."*

Rich attributes the investment in this team to be a key part of the firm's ability to grow ARR significantly in the past year and double the number of new enterprise logos.

If you are selling products alongside services, make sure that the sales engineers are deployed on opportunities where the seller actually intends to sell the product. One product leader whose team includes a go-to-market support/sales engineer shared that he was getting tied up doing demos for consultants who had no intention of selling the product to the client. They were just demo-ing the tool to showcase the internal capabilities they had.

Your sales channel decision should determine how much you invest in sales support roles. If your sellers are more high-level strategists with less product expertise, sales engineers can be a very smart investment.

Early in the product's maturity, product managers can and should fill this role. They're the only ones with both the market and product understanding. Just be careful that the product managers realize they are wearing a different hat when doing sales support, and they cannot conduct a sales call the same way they do during market research. Also make sure they sell the product's current feature set and don't fall into the trap of saying yes or promising every feature a customer asks about.

This is another reason why hiring commercially minded product leaders (versus technical specialists) will make new product launches easier. A commercially savvy product leader who supports your sellers effectively and helps them hit their goals will increase sellers' confidence in your productization strategy and trust in the product team.

SDRs

You may get to the point where it makes sense to invest in creating a sales development representative (SDR) role. One benefit of productizing is that more standardized services or products can be prequalified SDRs, rather than more expensive account executives or doer-sellers. SDRs focus on the initial stages of the sales process and specialize in generating and qualifying leads, making the first contact with potential customers, and setting up meetings or calls for the account executives who close the sales. The primary goal of an SDR team is to streamline the sales funnel, ensuring that the more experienced sales personnel can focus on high-probability opportunities and closing deals. This is incredibly valuable as you scale your go-to-market and want to leverage your sellers' time more cost-effectively.

For example, when TalentTether productized, they realized that their salespeople could be much more productive with SDRs supporting them. They built the team gradually, hiring SDRs instead of salespeople, as salespeople turned over as well as a small management layer to manage the SDRs. This approach enabled them to test, learn, and optimize their approach with limited up-front investment.

Whether you decide to invest in creating a SDR role or not, think carefully about how you will take all the great work that you did earlier in identifying your ICP(s) and ensuring that your sellers have a steady flow of leads that match your ICP and are focusing their time on those prospects.

Channel Partner

Collaborating with another organization that is selling products or services adjacent to yours can be a highly effective approach to market and distribute your new product or productized service. By leveraging your partner's existing relationships and resources, you can expand your market reach and access new customer segments. The channel partner can be a distributor, reseller, vendor, or another entity that adds value to the sales process. It works best when the partner is running out of new things to sell their target market and the cross-sell opportunity is relatively obvious.

For example, when AMEND Consulting created Batched (a SaaS-based dynamic production scheduling tool for the packaging printing industry), it partnered with Label Traxx, an established business management software provider for the packaging industry. Batched could be sold as an "add-on" to the Label Traxx software or as part of a comprehensive bundle.

It's an important strategy to consider, especially if there are established providers of complementary services. And, if there are established providers, neglecting a channel can be detrimental.

For example, one organization we worked with came to us because they were concerned that a new product they launched failed to gain market traction and rekindle growth like they expected. After doing "voice of the customer" research, we discovered that the core offering, although best in its class as an HR technology point solution, neglected to integrate with key customer channels—namely the HRIS and benefits administration platforms. Buyers expressed that they are looking to consolidate onto fewer platforms. Even if the core platform had an inferior solution to this problem, it was integrated out-of-the box and at no extra cost. So immediately, the problem is no longer urgent and expensive to buyers, and a great point solution has a huge uphill battle, and they certainly cannot charge a premium price. We advised the customer that no number of new features would solve this core channel problem. They needed to focus on integrations and single-sign-on first. Wisely, they acquired a company with strong technical architecture that helped accelerate their path to integrations and rekindle growth.

If you use a channel partner plus maintain your own sales force, you'll need to think through how to manage any conflict between the two. Conflicts between a channel partner and a company's own salesforce typically arise due to competition over customer accounts, unclear role definitions, and discrepancies in pricing or commission structures. Both teams might compete for the same sales, leading to potential revenue losses or conflicts over who "owns" the customer relationship.

To manage these conflicts effectively, it helps to clearly define territories and target customer segments and to create a commission structure that rewards both parties fairly and encourages collaboration rather than competition. This might include setting up joint incentives or bonus structures for deals where both the salesforce and channel partners collaborate effectively.

You'll also need to invest in training your channel partners. In the example of Finit (leading OneStream implementor), they must work alongside the sales organization for OneStream. OneStream sales needed to be educated about the OneStream PartnerPlace solutions that Finit developed, and that Finit offered more than just implementation services. Part of this also meant that they had to change the perception of which customers Finit best served, moving from just large enterprise customers to being able to deliver economic value to small and mid-market organizations.

Keep in mind that you have less pipeline control with channel partners, which is why so many organizations decide to have channel partners in addition to their own sales teams.

E-commerce

Some organizations may have products that can be sold via an e-commerce channel. B2B products or services suited for e-commerce sales are typically standardized and not overly complex, making it easy for customers to understand and purchase them without much direct sales interaction. A clear and straightforward pricing structure is crucial, as is the ability for the product or service to be delivered digitally or frequently reordered. Products that don't require a high degree of personal selling or customization, such as some software subscriptions or reports or training, are also ideal for e-commerce platforms.

In addition to being easier to scale, e-commerce channels typically allow companies to reach a wider audience. For example, e-commerce opens international markets. If designed well, e-commerce platforms often provide a seamless, self-service customer experience, which is increasingly preferred by business buyers. It allows customers to explore products, make decisions, and purchase at their convenience. An e-commerce channel can also be a way to sell lower priced step-on products to new customers and to sell lower-priced products that are not large enough to be a priority for salespeople to sell.

For example, Wolters Kluwer provides professional services and software solutions primarily to legal and healthcare sectors. They use an e-commerce channel to allow direct purchasing of some of their standardized solutions, like tax and accounting software, making it easier for clients to acquire and start using their products with minimal direct interaction.

Finally, selling through an e-commerce platform enables the collection of detailed data on customer behavior, preferences, and purchasing patterns. This data can be used to optimize marketing strategies, improve product offerings, and tailor customer interactions.

For example, Mercer offers reports online as both a way to attract new customers and to serve existing clients. The channel generates revenue, but its strategic value lies in providing insights about potential needs at existing clients or prospects who have never purchased anything else from Mercer.

This is an interesting consideration for B2B services firms because the e-commerce channel starts to straddle marketing, product, and sales. If strategically important enough, we suggest having a growth marketer be part of the e-commerce channel team.

Regardless of which channel strategy you pursue, you are almost likely going to have to sell through multiple channels.

Managing Multiple Channels

Many organizations who successfully productize eventually land on a hybrid or multichannel approach. They may have a dedicated product sales team and channel partners that sell to market segments that are less interested in services, and doer-sellers or dedicated services sellers who sell bundled solutions. They may have small pilot teams who only test and sell brand-new products and more mature teams who have multiple products and solutions in their bag.

One challenge of the multichannel approach is to ensure that clients, especially those who purchase more traditional services plus products or productized services, have an integrated experience. There is a risk that the introduction of product sellers into existing relationships managed by account managers or doer-sellers can lead to conflicts and can also overload a client with contacts and possibly make you look uncoordinated. For example, one chief revenue officer recounted,

> *"As we were transforming from a complete services company to having a mix of services and products, our buyer was still the same. Unfortunately, we had created two separate go-to-market organizations—one for services and one for products—and the client experience was terrible. It took us two to three years to realize this created confusion and frustration for customers (as well as us) and to create a more integrated approach."*

If you are selling to the same buyer, you may have a new integrated services and product go-to-market motion that replaces the old one entirely. This could be joint-selling or team-selling, for example.

Having an integrated client experience is part of the reason why TalentTether* decided not to add additional sales channels but instead invest in sales engineers. One former executive shared,

> *"Most of our best customers were global and had a different point of contact in each country because employment laws are varied around the world. We didn't want to layer on another point of contact per product or else the complexity of working with us would be too high. Also, part of our differentiation was we had sellers who could have an elevated and consultative conversation with the chief human resources officer, and we wanted to keep that. So, rather than creating a product sales team, we brought in sales engineers. It added some costs to the sale, but it was worth it to have product experts who could come in and design the solution or talk about the specifics of the individual product."*

Multiple channels typically also need their own messaging. For example, an HR consulting firm that we work with has doer-sellers, dedicated product sellers, and channel partners. Adding to the complexity is that some of the bundled solutions cross practice areas, such as HR technology and leadership development. One firm leader shared the challenge of this complexity:

> *"It's great that our value propositions cross silos and speak to board-level priorities like the future of work, but it is very difficult for our operating model. When a new solution or product goes live, it might be as relevant for our senior*

---

*   Pseudonym

consultants in one practice area as it is for our dedicated product sellers, or as it might be for our senior consultants in a completely different practice area. The enablement and messaging should be very different for each because how you position it for one buyer might be very different from how you would position it for a different buyer. It creates more layers of work."

Assembling Your Team

There are many resources available on how to build a sales team, including how to sequence hires (e.g., when to hire head of sales versus account executives versus sales operations[61]), how to design roles, hiring tactics, and the different sales skills you need at different stages of maturity (e.g., proven superstar who dislikes process at start-up versus team performer at scale-up)[62]. *How to Get to $10m in ARR and Beyond* by Jacco Van Der Kooij is a great resource for this.

Rather than summarizing that well-trodden material, we want to discuss (1) how the skills required to successfully sell products or productized services are different from the skills required to sell more customized services, and (2) how the skills you need to sell bundled solutions are different from the skills needed to just sell products or just sell customized services. This will help you decide if you need to retrain or upskill existing staff or bring in new skills.

Skills for Selling Products versus Customized Services

One marketing agency CEO confessed, "Our biggest challenge in successfully selling our products is that our salespeople don't know how to disagree with clients and explain why our standardized products are better than a custom engagement."

This is because when you are selling a customized service, you are focused on understanding customer needs and then convincing a customer that your organization has the capabilities to meet those needs. Customers are buying the promise that the people will be able to meet their needs. It's "Yes-as-a-Service.'"

It will be near impossible to successfully productize if you don't know how to say no to clients who request custom solutions but could be just as well served through a more productized approach. For example, a chief product officer of a training firm shared,

> *"It was very difficult to transform our sellers from relationship sellers to insight sellers. That shift is still hard because if you are teaching a customer why our productized solution is better, you must be willing to push back on what the customer is telling you. And that is uncomfortable for a lot of sellers. A lot of sellers just want to say yes and think it's going to lead to a deal."*

DCM Insights, a sales effectiveness research and training firm, has found that if you are selling a product, value-based selling methods such as Challenger are most effective. But when you are selling yourself and your advice, an approach called The Activator, characterized by proactive network building and collaboration, is the most effective. A contrarian, Challenger-like approach falls short when the person doing the selling is the product[63].

The ability to persuade customers that your solution meets their needs is a key component of the product selling skillset. One chief revenue officer observed,

> *"Customers will come up with all sorts of things that they think are best for them. But they don't know what's best for them. So, they might think that a bespoke solution where they've defined everything is going to give them the best outcome. Their experience of solving that problem is just what they have seen in the job they are in right there; they're not experts in the solution, only their pain. They don't have many reference points.*

You need sellers who are confident in saying, 'We have a strong understanding of your needs and we work with hundreds of customers who have the same problem and we already have something which achieves 80 percent of what you're trying to do, and it is tried and tested and works and we can adapt it slightly to cover 90 percent of your needs.' It reminds me of the Henry Ford quote. 'If I had asked people what they wanted, they would have said faster horses.'"

Selling Bundled Solutions

Selling bundled solutions that include both products and services requires a nuanced set of sales skills, often blending and enhancing the traditional skills used for selling products and services individually. A key skill is the ability to understand and articulate the combined value of products and services. This demands a deep comprehension of how the individual components of the bundle complement each other and create a holistic solution that addresses a broader range of the customer's needs. Sellers must be adept at consultative selling, where they act more as advisors who analyze customer problems and provide comprehensive solutions rather than just selling a product or service.

Compared to selling products alone, which focuses on benefits and possibly features and price, selling bundles requires integrating these elements with the intangible aspects of services such as customer support, customization, and ongoing relationships. This requires strong analytical skills to align the features of the product with the service components that enhance its value. One mistake we see is hiring product people to solution sell, where subject matter expertise/knowledge of the customer experience is more important.

On the other hand, selling services alone generally revolves around trust, credibility, and relationship-building, as services are intangible and often judged based on the provider's reputation and the customer's experience. Selling bundles successfully, therefore, combines these skill sets: the product knowledge and persuasiveness required for product sales with the relationship management and problem-solving skills crucial for selling services.

Sellers with experience in both product and service environments who have bundled solutions experience are not easy to find, which is why many organizations decide to take a team approach to selling bundled solutions.

Develop or Hire?

We are often asked whether existing sellers can develop the skills needed to sell more productized offerings. It depends on a lot of factors including what you are selling (e.g., bundled solutions, standalone products, etc.), your target market (existing clients, completely new market segment), whether you are building a new channel, and the speed at which you want to go.

Certainly, developing current team members has the advantage of leveraging their deep understanding of the company's culture, processes, and client base, which is invaluable if you are selling to your existing market. However, if the current team's skill gap is substantial or if speed to market is critical, hiring new salespeople who already possess experience and success in similar product-oriented environments is often more effective.

Many organizations choose to hire a sales pacesetter (or, typically, a group of pacesetters), bringing on new talent to model new behavior and set a new pace. For example, when Strategy Execution launched their subscription product, they hired a new sales director to lead the initial effort who had experience selling subscription products. Matthew Ansbro, former CRO of Strategy Execution, shared,

> *"We had to bring new people in to get people who had experience selling subscription products like SaaS but also to*

get people who had a different mindset, were confident in the strategy, and were living proof that there is a different way to sell. A lot of sales is about confidence, particularly if you are using more of a Challenger sales model where you are going to work to change clients' minds. The confidence of the new sellers was infectious and helped the rest of the team believe that the strategy would work. Without injecting new blood into the team, it is hard to get an existing organization to change. You might get one or two that change, but it's going to take you a lot longer."

These new hires can inject fresh perspectives and expertise into your team, potentially accelerating the transition and fostering a more dynamic sales culture. Additionally, new sales talent can serve as mentors or role models to existing staff, catalyzing a quicker and more organic skill development across the team. Balancing these approaches—investing in existing sellers while strategically adding new skills through hiring—can create a robust, adaptable sales force that is well-equipped to thrive in a market that increasingly values integrated solutions.

As with any strategic change, if you are using your existing sales channel, some turnover is likely. One CPO of a leadership training company that sunset their customized training offerings shared,

"We had a lot of turnover because we changed the job of the seller significantly. We went from the seller being a consultant seller where they created their own solution to being a product seller, leading with insight and selling a standard solution. Some people voluntarily left and a couple of people tried but just could never get any traction."

Similarly, when TalentTether* transformed their go-to-market strategy, they created separate roles for hunters (to bring in new customers) and farmers (account managers to retain and expand existing clients). For the first time, the firm created quotas for the hunter sales roles rather than just paying pure commission, which helped people self-select who did not have the right skill set to successfully hunt. The former head of sales enablement shared,

> *"Initially, a lot of the legacy sales team wanted to be hunters. We knew it wasn't the right answer for some people, but we let them self-select their path. When our sellers saw their quotas and did the math to understand the pacing required to meet role expectations, several people put their hands up and said, 'I think I made a mistake.' We helped those individuals transition into farmer territories better suited for their skills and they appreciated the agency afforded them during a significant transformation."*

Mindset and Behavior Change

If you are using your existing sales channel to sell, either as the sole channel or to complement existing channels, upskilling is not your only challenge. Often, it is the mindset and the behaviors of the existing sellers that is the largest hurdle to overcome.

As we discussed in our book *Fearless: How to Transform a Services Culture and Successfully Productize*, many change management challenges surrounding productization are rooted in fear. And not just fear of change but fear of saying no, fear of failure, fear of cannibalization, and fear of disruption.

For example, fear of cannibalizing current services or products can kill our best products before they even have a chance to succeed. This

---

*   Pseudonym

is particularly acute when you have lower-priced products being sold alongside higher-priced services and commission structures treat both the same. Sellers want to protect their services revenue, so they may not introduce products if they compete with the services.

This fear is derived from scarcity thinking, which feeds the fear that new products will cannibalize revenue from existing, higher-priced services. For many professional services organizations, scarcity thinking is the modus operandi. The time and resources you sell are, by nature, limited. The concept of scarcity mindset is rooted in both psychology and neurology and describes the phenomena of being unable to escape the consequences of thinking about scarce resources.

Another fear driven by scarcity thinking, especially with doer-sellers, is the fear of being "disrupted" by having their personal expertise and relationships be less relevant in a more productized organization. The CEO of a management consulting firm that ultimately decided to abandon its productization efforts confided,

> *"The root cause of our failure was fear. Our team had defined their identities by their work and, for the past ten years, that work had been developing customized solutions for each client. Now we were telling our consultants that their work—their identities—were going to be productized. They kept insisting that a standardized solution would not meet client needs, but at the root, they were afraid of losing their identities."*

A product leader at another large consulting firm added,

> *"When a product or a product feature set appears to solve the same client problem as a consulting service, consulting leaders are much more likely to try to kill it. I'm always stunned because if I can figure out how to productize this, another company can also do it. And instead of saying, 'Build that, and we'll consult on different issues,' they try and prevent it from*

being built. But it's only a matter of time before somebody else creates a similar product that doesn't require any consulting. There's resistance to products that might be a replacement to consulting knowledge."

To successfully productize, most organizations need to see the opportunity for more. More options, more market segments, more resources. In other words, organizations that want to successfully productize need to cultivate abundance thinking.

Abundance thinking also helps productizing services firms recognize that productization doesn't necessarily limit clients' willingness or ability to grow their spending and, in fact, that it is possible to sell both services and products to clients. This helps you overcome the fear that a product strategy might cannibalize services revenue. And a willingness to risk cannibalization has been found to be a key driver of innovative cultures[64].

Another fear is the fear of saying no. The experience of one C-level executive at a research and development services firm shows how fear at all levels of the organization can thwart productization. He diagnosed the root cause of their productization challenges as coming from both a fear of saying no—to short-term revenue and to clients:

"The problem that runs up and down the organization is a fear of saying no. Salespeople, account people—almost everyone. Product people want to say no to one-off customization requests, but they get slapped on the wrist if they do. They don't want to be seen as someone just saying no. We believe the client is happier if they say yes."

Many professional services organizations pride themselves on their ability to meet every customer request. But when building a scalable product, you cannot say yes to everything. Where teams get stuck is that saying no is hard and they don't want to do it. It is largely driven by the fear of upsetting that customer and losing them.

With an abundance mindset, you may realize there are a few alternatives to customer requests for customization. First, you understand that the right response is not "no" but "why?" so that you can discover if there is a root to the request that could benefit all customers. Next, in an abundance mindset you recognize that sometimes you need to fire a customer that does not fit your organization's strategy to scale. For example, when Sean led the product function for CultureIQ, the organization was transitioning from a tech-enabled services organization with a white-glove model for configuring the survey platform and analyzing results to a SaaS platform model that included standard survey program offerings that could be run self-service. There were a few large customers who didn't want to transition until there was "full parity" with every configuration option. Eventually, organizational leaders realized that it was okay to endure the short-term pain of losing a few big customers and that a better business would be only serving customers who are happy with a standard solution.

Finally, there may also be skepticism about the strategy of productization and fear of failure, especially if the organization has tried productizing before and was not successful.

Winning Hearts and Minds—Communication

When an organization is struggling to gain buy-in for the product strategy, it is often because the leaders have not created or communicated a compelling and realistic vision for the strategy. Pursuing productization without a vision of what, why, and how you want to achieve can be extremely painful.

If your current sales channel is to sell the new products, you need to win the sales team's hearts and minds (along with aligning their compensation and upskilling them!). This requires a compelling and transparent explanation of how a strategy of offering standardized products supports your organization's mission and vision. You must explain the commercial relationship between services and products and clearly communicate the value proposition for existing clients and new customers. These conversations cannot occur just once; they need to happen over and over.

One of the key findings from research on transforming organizational culture is that if you want to change people's behaviors, you must change their beliefs. Change management researchers have found that employees respond to organizational change based on their readiness and motivation, both of which are tied to what they believe about the tasks they are being asked to perform and the organization they are being asked to perform them for. A transformational leader will need to foster belief changes en route to behavior change[65]. You change beliefs through education and storytelling, but you also change beliefs by personally demonstrating the new behaviors and discussing your own beliefs behind them.

As previously mentioned, confidence is extremely important to sales success. Celebrating early wins and creating visibility into how early deals were won can help with this.

Brian Joseph, CEO and founding partner of RevJen, a firm that provides nonprofits with executive peer groups and revenue generation training, found that he needed a few things to win the hearts and minds of his sales team. First, a compelling vision for how their products were going to help achieve the organization's mission. Second, a good list of beta customers and testimonials. Third, incentives that encouraged selling the most scalable products. Fourth, constant communication about the company, products, and emphasizing the vision. And fifth, clear guidance on the ideal customer life cycle. In other words, explaining his vision for how a customer would buy one product, and then another, and then potentially, future products or services. Defining the ideal customer life cycle requires us to define which products are good introductory products and which products should be reserved for add-ons or cross-sell.

Winning Hearts and Minds—Co-Creation

At one large business process outsourcing firm, the financial operations management practice area serves nearly two hundred of the world's largest organizations. Within that practice, the account directors (ADs) are the ones responsible for the complete account, including the client relationship and often the hundreds of firm employees who help serve that account. For the successful inclusion and adoption of products within larger services contracts, it was vital for the product team to work closely with the ADs to make sure they felt heard and they understood how products supported the success of their accounts. To do that, the team created regular touchpoints with the AD council and coordinated all voice of the customer activities through these relationship owners.

During Initial Product Development

As a way of not just winning hearts and minds but also gathering valuable insights into market needs (and customer reactions), ask for seller feedback during the product innovation process. The opportunity to provide feedback will make the sales team feel more invested in the product and more equipped to sell it.

Unfortunately, many product managers and developers underestimate the value that the people in existing go-to-market functions (e.g., sellers, marketing, account management) can bring to the product ideation and development process. Or they fear that, if consulted, sellers will block access to their customers for market research (which does happen) or, if included in market research conversations, their customers will hijack the conversation and turn it into a commercial conversation. If you have real evidence to support this fear, then we recommend recording the calls for sellers to watch and using interviews as a chance to collect information that celebrates the successes of the sellers. We also hear product leaders complain about "too many cooks in the kitchen," to which we gently remind them that complex stakeholder management is a large part of their job.

If you are developing a bundled solution, it will be critical to have service sales and delivery as part of the product creation process to make sure that the products will integrate as seamlessly as possible with the more customized services. For example, Sean likes to use service delivery staff and sellers as customer-proxies in product testing. They are much easier to access quickly, provide great insights to also what will work for the business, and they turn the internal testers into co-conspirators from a change management perspective. There's really no excuse for not using your internal experts as early testers.

Moreover, the product leader should have regular check-ins with sales leaders and account executives to provide their feedback on the product road map priorities. It should be easy for sellers to forward every single customer request/conversation into the product team's insights tracking. That data should then be used to explain why the product is prioritized the way it is.

Unfortunately, we have seen organizations that, because of a desire for speed and/or a fear of the legacy business quashing new products, developed their products in a vacuum and then were unable to benefit from a bundled solution sales approach. A consulting leader at one such firm shared a cautionary tale.

> *"At first, consulting didn't have a strong enough advocate for them on the product team, so the product was not designed to make it operationally benefit services clients. We did not have a mechanism where the people who were expected to sell, the consultants, could include their priorities on the development*

plan. It took us three long years to develop a product that worked well with existing services."

After Launch

It's also important to iterate. Build into the plan the time to evaluate market feedback, marketing tools, sales pitch, and the product features with sellers, and then refresh collateral and the product if needed. Ask the sales team what's working, what needs to be revised, and what additional research is needed to better understand the customers or the market landscape.

Samantha Polovina, partner and global product category leader over Mercer's TAAP product, has been able to increase the product's annual growth rate from just 5 percent to more than 25 percent by building a strong network of internal product ambassadors among the client-facing consulting and account management teams and investing in those relationships. She shared,

> *"The client managers know they have an open channel to provide me with their feedback about the product. The more I show them that we are listening to them and evolving the product accordingly, the more likely they are to present it to their clients."*

Lastly, someone from the sales team should also sit on the Product Governance Council* if you've put one in place. Keeping the conversations flowing to and from the sales team will lead to a better

---

* The Product Governance Council conducts regular product reviews. These reviews provide an opportunity to assess the performance of the product portfolio, evaluate new product ideas, and make informed decisions about resource allocation. Additionally, product reviews hold teams accountable, ensure alignment across the organization, and help prioritize the right ideas in the pipeline. We cover this in-depth in our book *Fearless: How to Transform a Services Culture and Successfully Productize.*

understanding of customer needs; moreover, that back and forth sharing of ideas will also help you to win the hearts of your sales team.

Creating a Compelling Sales Compensation Plan

You'll need to give careful thought to the compensation plans for sales channel(s) to ensure they intelligently support your productization strategy. One CEO of an IT consulting firm recently shared with us, "We need to restructure our incentive plan. Our leaders and consultants are all incented on short-term revenue growth, which is making it very hard to get traction with our new products that have lower price points but better margins and more revenue visibility."

A sales compensation plan can be structured into four main parts: base pay, variable pay, incentives, conditions. Variable pay links pay to performance, including commissions, which are a percentage of sales, and quotas, which are sales targets. This category also includes payout percentages and caps to manage earnings potential. Incentives like SPIFs* and bonuses encourage focus on specific goals or exceptional performance. Finally, conditions such as claw backs, accelerators, and decelerators adjust the plan based on business needs and market conditions, ensuring that the compensation structure aligns with company strategies and manages risks effectively.

Many resources are available on sales compensation strategy and structure from organizations like Gartner, SBI Growth, Insight Revenue, and more. We won't go into deep detail of dos and don'ts for designing sales compensation plans. Our goal here is to give you some perspective on how other B2B services firms have grappled with the challenge of designing and changing sales compensation plans that support their productizations strategy.

---

*   (Sales Performance Incentive Fund) is a short-term sales incentive designed to drive immediate focus on specific products or goals. For example, a $5,000 bonus to sales reps for each new enterprise-level client they secure during a quarter.

Also, this is only about sales compensation. Incentives across many functions will need to be revisited if you want to be successful, and we cover this extensively in our previous book *Fearless: How to Transform a Services Culture and Successfully Productize*, chapter 7.

Two big challenges we see especially with doer-seller channels or channels that also sell services is balancing focus and encouraging product sales, especially when product price points may be lower than services. For example, one consulting firm leader candidly shared,

> *"Our consultants have no incentive right now to include products in their services engagements. The only ones who do are equity partners who realize the strategic value of growing our product revenue."*

Encouraging Product Sales

If you have a sales channel that is selling both products and services, your compensation plan will need to ensure sellers are motivated to sell both products and services, even though the products may have lower price points. The compensation plan needs to carefully balance incentives to avoid overprioritizing one over the other.

Similarly, while bespoke services might bring in more revenue, lower-priced products are typically more profitable. If the product revenue is recurring, it will also be more valuable than non-recurring revenue. Aligning compensation to reward higher margin and/or recurring revenue rather than just revenue targets is crucial but can be complex to communicate and implement.

We recommend changing sales commissions to pay out a lower percentage on non-scalable services and a higher percentage on product sales to "move" employees in the right direction. This is also known as a carrot-and-stick approach (higher commission for productized and a new lowered commission for customized services). Christoffer Ellehuus, the former CEO of Strategy Execution, shared how he changed incentives for the sales team during his company's product transition. Salespeople received a 3 percent commission on consulting engagements and 6 percent on higher gross margin, recurring revenue subscription product sales. The sales commission for product sales was *twice* that of consulting sales. "It's not about telling people they can't do something. It's about putting enough barriers and meaningful incentives in place to move them in the direction you want," Christoffer said.

It's also interesting to note that Strategy Execution challenged sellers' notion that the overall revenue would be lower. As a reminder, the firm sold project management training services. While the productized training had a lower price per employee than the customized training, the go-to-market strategy was to encourage customers to spend the same but include more employees in the training. Their messaging was centered around "democratizing learning," which reinforced this strategy. Matthew Ansbro, chief revenue officer, shared, "Yes, the unit price would be lower, but rather than selling training for 30 people, we wanted to sell training for 1000 people to keep revenue the same if not higher."

Instead of traditional revenue-based commissions, some firms have implemented profit-based commissioning. This strategy directly ties the commission rate to the gross margin of the product or service sold. For instance, lower-ticket but high-margin solutions that are more productized might offer higher commission rates than high-ticket, low-margin solutions that are mostly customized services.

We have also seen success with multiyear commission structures for productized services that involve subscriptions or recurring revenue (like SaaS products). Commissions can be structured to pay out over multiple years, which encourages sellers to focus on the long-term value and retention of customers rather than just up-front contract values.

The strategic use of sales performance incentive funds (SPIFs) can promote new products or new markets. For instance, introducing tiered SPIFs that escalate with the number of new product units sold can create immediate and compelling incentives for sales teams to push productized offerings. Or SPIFs where they earn an extra point in commission once they bring in five new customers in an industry that has been flagged as an expansion market. They can also be useful for encouraging the sales of lower-priced step-on products that you may be using to penetrate a new market.

SPIFs can also be a way to incentivize sales of new products when you don't want to commit to an annual commission structure yet because you are still trying to validate the economics of the product (e.g., if you are still trying to validate the gross margin structure of a more productized approach and are concerned that your new sales commissions may be too high and could eliminate any economic return of incremental gross margin).

If your doer-sellers or services sellers are identifying product sales cross-sell opportunities with existing services clients and handing those leads over to a product sales team, you'll also need to think through how they are incented for generating those leads. One product leader at a large global consulting firm candidly shared that the incentives for their consultants to generate product leads was not "sweet" enough. She said, "The cross-sell incentives are too diluted. They only get credit for the first year of a multiyear subscription, and it does not feel worthwhile given the total size of their revenue goals."

This question of who gets credit and how credit is shared is a tricky one when you have multiple sales channels who will bring in bundled sales like doer-sellers plus a dedicated product sales team. If commissions are split too much, it may create a disincentive for a doer-seller to include a product in a sale, but organizations are also trying to avoid double or even triple counting sales so commission payouts do not overwhelm their customer acquisition cost assumptions. One consulting firm leader shared her frustration with her firm's split structure:

> *"If you're the consultant who's in charge, you are disincentivized from bringing anybody else into an engagement because suddenly what was 100 percent of your sales credit and delivery credit is now 50 percent. And then if you bring in another person from digital products, now you are sharing a third, a third, a third. The model isn't encouraging a team approach to win deals. To want to take a team approach, you must believe that instead of selling a $70,000 engagement or a $150,000 engagement, you're going to sell a $2 million deal. Half of $2 million is better than a hundred percent of $150,000. But that's a huge change in mindsets."*

Balancing Focus

If you are bundling products and services, you may have a more complex sales process (longer sales cycle, more stakeholders) than if you are selling standalone products or services and "compared to" services, so the compensation plan should acknowledge these differences in sales complexity and effort. For example, to encourage the sale of new productized offerings alongside traditional services, we have seen organizations introduce bonuses for selling bundled packages. This not only boosts product sales but also maintains the attractiveness of service contracts. For example, a salesperson might receive a higher total commission or bonus for selling a combined package of products and services than for selling each component separately.

There's also a risk that incentivizing product sales might cannibalize more lucrative service contracts if not structured properly. It's important to design a plan that complements the sales of both, perhaps by creating bundled offers or cross-selling incentives.

Simon Frewer, former CEO of Challenger, shared that when they launched their subscription product, "It was a real challenge to figure out how to come up with a comp plan that rewards selling in the lower initial price subscription product but doesn't over reward it so much that they don't sell the $4 million project for the $200K subscription."

This is particularly challenging when the product is supposed to grow the revenue pie, not just the profit margin pie. One consulting leader candidly shared, "We didn't want to make the product sales goals too big because we still needed the consulting revenues. We had to sweeten the product sales compensation enough so that products would always be included with services but not so much that services revenue started to decline."

One way to address this is to have accelerators that reward balanced sales portfolios. Consider a consulting company that is introducing a suite of software products designed to enhance the efficiency of these services. In the base compensation plan, sales representatives earn a 5 percent commission on consulting service contracts and a 10 percent commission on software product sales due to the products' higher margins. To incentivize a balanced approach to sales, the company introduces an accelerator: if a sales representative meets 100 percent of their quota for both service contracts and software sales within a quarter, they activate an accelerator. This accelerator increases their commission rates by 20 percent for all additional sales above the quota for the rest of that quarter. Therefore, commissions for services rise from 5 percent to 6 percent, and commissions for software sales increase from 10 percent to 12 percent.

Additionally, to further promote balanced sales portfolios, the company offers an end-of-year bonus. If a representative's sales consistently achieve a 70/30 split between services and products throughout the fiscal year, they receive a bonus equivalent to 10 percent of their total annual commissions.

Another tactic we have seen is to set specific quotas for product sales versus services sales. For example, one sales leader shared, "Most sellers will get to their quota however they need to, unless it is prescribed that the overall sales number has to be a particular mix like 80 percent services and 20 percent product."

Timing of Changes

Changing a sales compensation structure is a critical decision that can significantly affect the motivation and performance of your sellers. Aligning changes with the end of the fiscal year can help in seamless integration into annual planning and budgeting processes.

Communicating upcoming changes to sales commission structures well in advance is crucial for maintaining transparency and building trust with your sellers. Early notification allows sellers enough time to adapt their strategies and develop necessary skills, particularly if they are selling more productized solutions for the first time. It also provides an opportunity for feedback. It's important to continually explain the longer-term strategic vision underlying the changes and demonstrate how the changes will benefit both the team and company in the long run.

To ensure a smooth transition, consider involving key team members in the planning stages and possibly phasing in major adjustments. Effectively enabling your sellers with training, great collateral, and tools can address concerns and clarify how sellers can thrive under the new compensation structure. Monitoring the effects post-implementation and being willing to adjust are also very important.

Speaking of flexibility, if you have a new product launch in the middle of the fiscal year, a SPIF can be a good tool to incent those sales for the rest of the fiscal year. SPIFs can also be used to address unintended consequences from your commission structure. For example, we were working with one organization who thought that there was a risk that their doer-sellers would generate low-quality product leads for the product sales team. They decided to manage this risk by implementing a SPIF for one quarter on the product leads and test whether lead quality degraded with the additional incentive. They used conversion rates of leads to assess lead quality. After determining that lead quality did not degrade, they replaced the SPIF with a permanent commission structure on the leads for the next fiscal year.

Uncertainty around unintended consequences of commission and bonus structures is another reason why we recommend doing pilots before full scale launch with the broader team of sellers. You do not need to be 100 percent confident in your assumptions, but somewhere between the classic 40/70 rule* is a good basis for moving on from a pilot.

Thinking About Sales Compensation During Product Design

Timing of a sales compensation change is different from timing of sales compensation design. Ideally, you are considering sales compensation design when you are making your initial business case for a product.

Assumptions about the economics of a product idea, including utilization rates, renewal rates, customer acquisition costs, and commissions, all need to be part of the initial business plan before a product is even developed. For example, one CEO shared,

> *"It was important that we knew ahead of time that we were going to lose a lot of money in year one because we were going to buy market share in the form of the very high first year commissions we would be paying. Our plan was to make it up in year two through renewals. We could have bought market*

---

* The 40/70 rule is a decision-making principle that Colin Powell, the former US Secretary of State and Chairman of the Joint Chiefs of Staff, famously used. According to this rule, Powell believed that you should have between 40 percent and 70 percent of the information you need to decide. If you have less than 40 percent, you likely don't have enough data to make an informed choice. If you have more than 70 percent, you may be waiting too long and missing opportunities for action.

*share through lower prices rather than high commissions, but
we did not want to risk losing our customers when we raised
prices to become profitable. So we stayed competitive with our
pricing but maximally motivated our sellers."*

Promotion Criteria May Need to Shift

If one of your primary sales channels for your more productized
offerings is a doer-seller channel, then you will also need to revisit
your promotion criteria. In many professional services organizations,
promotion decisions for doer-sellers, especially at the partner level, are
heavily weighted by the amount of top-line revenue that they bring
in and/or manage.

If, however, you are going to market with more productized
solutions that have lower annual revenue and have only adjusted
compensation structures but *not* promotion criteria, you may not see
a change in doer-seller behavior.

One consulting firm leader confided,

> *"It's bad for people who are going up for promotion because
> we traditionally look at both sales and delivery credits for
> promotion decisions. But right now, if a consultant sells a
> product, they get a partial sales credit, the product sales team
> gets the other part, and they get zero delivery credit. Our split
> credit model creates a disincentive for them to bring anyone
> else into the sale. If you keep cutting your sales credit in half,
> every time you sell a bundled product-service solution to a
> client, you end up having to sell to twice as many clients. Even
> if they get a special incentive compensation kicker for selling
> the product, they don't get the credits they need to be eligible for
> promotion. Our consultants don't just want the cash, they want
> the promotion."*

Sales Effectiveness

As you are validating go-to-market fit, you will also start investing in sales effectiveness capabilities, an umbrella term for the efforts aimed at improving the efficiency and success of your sellers.

Under this umbrella are many things that you may already have such as a sales playbook and sales operations to manage the technology (i.e., CRM system) and processes such as territory design, lead scoring, and analytics that enable salespeople to be efficient and effective. It also includes sales enablement activities, which ensure that sales teams have the necessary product or services knowledge, material, and skills to engage effectively with customers and lead management such as prospecting, scheduling appointments, and qualifying leads that marketing has generated.

Most B2B services organizations that are productizing already have many of these capabilities. The challenge is that they have been designed for selling *services* rather than *products*. For example, CRM systems must be modified to handle products, and accurately forecasting sales for new products can be challenging due to a lack of historical data. Sales operations will need to develop new metrics and models to predict product sales performance. Sales enablement tools and platforms may need to be adapted or replaced to support product selling activities such as demo tools.

If your current sales channel is mostly doer-sellers, sales effectiveness capabilities tend to be very immature in addition to being geared toward services selling. For example, organizations who sell primarily through doer-sellers typically do not have sales playbooks or have strong sales enablement capabilities. There may also be very little lead management support or guidance.

If you are building these capabilities from scratch, you may want to consider hiring a fractional revenue operations executive (or agency) to help structure your CRM, lead lists, and reporting dashboards. We suggest doing this before investing in a dedicated product sales team so that when you do start to hire new sellers, they will be effective. It is harder to build sales effectiveness infrastructure after your team is in place, which is why we recommend starting to build it early, even if you are outsourcing it at first[66]. There are *many* existing resources on how to create strong sales effectiveness capabilities, and we have made some of our favorite tools available for you at *www.commercialize.book.com*.

Key Takeaways

1. Selling a customized service and selling a more standardized product are two very different things. The divide between selling a custom solution and selling a scalable product is a large one.

2. Organizations often need a different sales team or channel to sell products. For example, the economics of a product sale are different (typically lower price point but higher margin and higher lifetime value) and rely heavily on lead generation and value-based selling techniques like demonstrating how a prospect would solve their challenges with a productized offering, sales techniques that services sellers may not have experience using.

3. Successfully selling your new products or productized services is not as simple as winning the hearts and minds of your existing sellers. Selling productized offerings is an opportunity to create new sales roles and sell through new channels.

4. There are four types of sales channels: product-led, people, e-commerce, partners. The different types of people sellers include doer-sellers, services sellers, and dedicated products sellers.

5. Sales channel decisions should be guided by productization strategy and maturity.

6. If you are selling to the same buyer, you may have a new integrated services and product go-to-market motion that replaces the old services selling approach entirely.

7. If you have a sales channel that is selling both products and services, your compensation plan will need to ensure sellers are motivated to sell both products and services, even though the products may have lower price points. The compensation plan needs to carefully balance incentives to avoid overprioritizing one over the other.

8. If you are bundling products and services, you may have a more complex sales process (longer sales cycle, more stakeholders), than if you are selling standalone products or services and "compared to" services, so the compensation plan should acknowledge these differences in sales complexity and effort.

Additional Resources

✗ Product sales executive job descriptions

✗ Sales playbook template

✗ Sales funnel math tool to set targets

✗ Key principles for enabling sales team members

✗ Sales training deck for new product template

✗ Competitor talking points and decision-tree template

✗ Product demo best practices and sample outline

(Please download the tools at www.commercializebook.com)

PLANNING FOR RENEWALS FROM DAY ONE

We recently got a call from the CEO of a US-based company specializing in bespoke data analysis for the retail sector. Two years earlier they had launched a subscription-based analytics platform designed to provide real-time insights for small- to medium-sized retail businesses.

Initially it was a hit.

The platform provided powerful analytics tools, including predictive modeling and customer behavior analysis, which were typically only accessible to larger retailers with deep pockets. However, within two years, renewal rates were far below the assumptions in the initial business case and below average for similar products. It was a "leaky bathtub"; they could attract new customers, but the customers did not stay. The envisioned scale and profitability failed to materialize.

After diving into the platform and how it was supported, we saw a few problems explaining the high customer churn rate:

1. Recurring Impact: After the initial onboarding and first few months of use, customers noticed that the data insights became predictable and less impactful. The firm missed an

opportunity to make the analytics more valuable over time. As more data was collected, they could have designed a platform that provided increasingly accurate predictions and insights, but they didn't.

2. Underinvestment in Customer Success: The firm had underestimated the importance of continuous customer support and success initiatives. Clients found themselves navigating the complex toolset of the platform with minimal support, leading to frustration and underutilization of the platform.

In a candid interview, the CEO reflected on the experience:

"It's like we built a luxury liner but scrimped on the crew and the maintenance it needed to journey successfully. We've learned that the value isn't just in the launch; it's in the increasing impact and continuous support you provide along the way."

It is a common failure point we see with most new-to-productization organizations. They *want* their products to be renewable, but they don't plan for it, both in design of the product as well the go-to-market strategy. In this chapter, we'll discuss some of the specific challenges B2B services companies face when trying to develop more renewable business models as well as some of the basics of creating a customer success capability.

Renewal Intent versus Renewal Design

In the past three years, we have assessed the productization maturity[*] of more than two hundred professional services organizations that

---

[*] The Vecteris Productize Maturity Diagnostic™ (https://www.vecteris.com/diagnostic) assesses an organization's effectiveness across twenty-six product innovation measurements and internal education, alignment, and management activities. It is used for benchmarking, prioritization, and performance management.

are trying to productize. In analyzing this rich data set, we found that managing customer experience post-sales is a weakness for most firms and the *lowest* scoring area for all the go-to-market capabilities.

It is understandable. **Most organizations *intend* for products to be renewable but don't properly *design* for renewal. They wrongly think that if they create a subscription pricing schema, they will have recurring revenue.**

In fact, **many B2B services organizations unintentionally design for churn instead of renewal from day one.** This trap is especially acute when our brains are trained on selling short-term engagements. Most B2B services organizations are built around projects. Their culture, mindset, systems, and compensation system all focus on projects or engagements. Yes, they want clients to sign up for more projects, but that is reoccurring revenue, not *recurring* revenue.

In a recurring revenue business, the mindset needs to shift from "how do I get the next project?" to "how do I fulfill the product promise in a way that the customer wants to renew and perhaps even grow the relationship?"

Even services firms who have had a retainer-based model can struggle with managing customer experiences post-product sales so that customers renew. This is because in a retainer-based model, the focus is typically on maintaining a steady level of service, ensuring client satisfaction on a continuous but relatively static basis. But product renewals, as we'll discuss, often require more dynamic monitoring of usage and ongoing product enhancements. For example, we worked with a marketing firm that traditionally operated on a retainer model. When it introduced a suite of customer behavior data products as part of its productized services, it had to expand focus to not only providing ongoing marketing services but also to ensuring that clients were effectively using the data, seeing the value, and continuing to subscribe to the data updates based on demonstrated ROI. This requires a different set of customer health analytics, customer support, and engagement strategies than those used in a purely service-oriented retainer model.

And it's not just B2B services organizations that make this mistake. Experts say that a key contributing factor to the SaaS crash of 2022 was a misunderstanding of the importance of the customer success (CS) function in the SaaS model[67]. Frank V. Cespedes, a senior lecturer at Harvard Business School, said, "When demand slows and there's a need to cut costs, firing a CS rep often feels like an 'easy' decision to many executives. 'After all, we already won the customer.' But CS affects revenue in . . . ways that, when combined, are usually bigger than cost savings from decreasing CS headcount."

In a business model where customer lifetime value is highly correlated with length of relationship, reducing churn and increasing customer retention by even a little usually has a disproportionate impact on lifetime value.

Go-to-Market Includes Designing for Renewals

As previously discussed, the bowtie analogy for extending a sales funnel is helpful to acknowledge the importance of post-sale engagement, customer success, and expansion after the point of sale. It highlights the dual focus of strong go-to-market strategies: not only acquiring new customers but also maximizing the value of existing ones. It underscores the significance of the entire customer life cycle, emphasizing that the relationship doesn't end at the sale but rather enters a new phase of growth and opportunity. Without post-sale engagement and customer success, the entire business model of a recurring revenue business won't be profitable. That said, whether or not you treat customer success as a sales center is a different decision (i.e. do customer success leaders carry quotas for renewal and expansion, or does that sit in a pure sales org?).

As such, a key part of the success of a renewable product is your strategy for retaining your clients that subscribe to your offering. As you are making decisions about product design, packaging, pricing, and positioning, you continuously ask how you are going to build sustainable, scalable value over time. Also, how do you turn those users into advocates for what you do to spread the word to potential expansion or cross-sell opportunities?

Customer Success Capabilities

From the day you land your very first product user, you'll need to decide who is responsible for ensuring that your customers are using the product.

When you are in the earlier stage of evaluating product-market fit, the product leader is playing the role of customer success, perhaps supported by a junior customer success resource.

A word about terms here. **Customer success** simply refers to a support system focused on helping customers get the most out of their products or productized services, including onboarding, troubleshooting, and regular check-ins. This role involves understanding a customer's business objectives and actively working toward helping them meet those goals.

In contrast, **customer support** typically focuses on immediate issue resolution. For example, if a software user encounters a bug or a malfunction, the support team steps in to solve this specific problem. Here, the interaction with the customer is usually transactional and limited to the scope of troubleshooting and fixing issues. The support team's priority is ensuring that the product functions as promised but not necessarily optimizing the customer's use of the product.

On the other hand, **account management** covers a broader spectrum but with different priorities. Account managers handle the overall relationship with the customer, including renewals and sales opportunities. They aim to maintain and grow revenue from the account through regular check-ins and by offering additional products or services. However, while they do focus on customer satisfaction, their approach isn't always tailored to ensure that the customer leverages the product to achieve specific business outcomes. Their activities are often driven by sales targets and the overall health of the account rather than the day-to-day success of the customer in using the product.

As organizations move from initial alpha/closed beta to validating go-to-market fit, we strongly suggest investing in more dedicated customer success to ensure that new customers are onboarded effectively, and that customers use and renew the offering. **We suggest this investment before dedicated sales hires.**

For example, when Challenger first launched their subscription platform, the advisory team was also playing the role of the customer success team. Simon Frewer, former CEO recounted,

> *"Having the advisory team as the initial customer success team worked well because they knew our product and content so well. They could point the customer to the product or, if we did not have content that was included in the product yet, they could also manually deliver it."*

Over time, however, you'll want a more dedicated customer success team who has a product-first orientation. This was also part of Challenger's journey. Simon shared,

> *"Because our advisors were super friendly and loved serving customers, they were perfectly happy to keep manually sending content rather than directing customers to the product. I knew if we wanted to change behavior and serve our customers more scalably through the product, we would need a new model."*

The job of customer success will be to onboard new customers and ensure they are effectively using the product. You'll need systems for managing ongoing customer relationships including tracking customer interactions, preferences, and feedback to ensure satisfaction and retention. You will also need to invest in analytics to understand customer usage patterns, preferences, and churn risks.

Depending on what your existing go-to-market strategy is today, designing for retention could be an evolution or full-scale revolution. For example, a leading sales consulting firm who went to market through doer-sellers launched a new digital platform that provides benchmarking, research, and on-demand coaching. Partners started dropping the product in as a line item in statements of work, and unsurprisingly, the product had over 90 percent churn. What the firm realized was that partners lacked any structure to methodically find, execute, and then renew product sales opportunities. They brought in a new vice president of sales and customer success whose first action was to create a playbook for managing the digital solution sales and renewal process and operating rhythm. Within several quarters, they had documented the predictable "winning moves" and signals that partners could use to efficiently sell and renew the opportunities. With minimal overhead, both growth and renewal rates of the digital platform skyrocketed.

If you have the budget, at the go-to-market validation phase (or even earlier depending on the capacity of your product leader), you'll want to hire a head or director of customer success. This leader will be responsible for defining the customer success strategy, processes, and team structure. Look for someone with prior experience in building customer success organizations, preferably in the B2B space and ideally in a product-led company.

You should also leverage your existing services team's customer-facing experience and domain knowledge. If you have a services professional who has been closely involved in the productization strategy or also has a product background, they could transition into a customer success role. For example, Zendesk, which started as a support ticketing service, built their customer success team by upskilling employees from their professional services organization[68].

If your go-to-market strategy includes bundling your products with services or even selling products alongside services, you'll need to make sure the customer success and delivery teams are well integrated.

Customer Success When Selling Bundled Services and Product Solutions

Some services organizations that have account managers who traditionally focus on service delivery and client satisfaction may decide to also add customer success responsibilities to those account managers. As they mature, however, they often decide to create separate customer success roles that focus on product adoption, usability, and the continual value these products bring to your clients. But BOTH teams will need to be well-versed in both the product's details and the service nuances so they can provide comprehensive support and provide a more cohesive user experience.

Organizations that do not have a services account management team but still want to bundle services with products typically need to develop a customer success function that can adopt a more consultative approach, where customer success staff act as business advisors. This means going beyond simple troubleshooting to understand the customer's business model and workflows deeply.

Regardless of the staffing model, product onboarding takes on new importance, evolving into a process that not only teaches clients how to use the products but also how these enhance the services they are already familiar with.

Customer success can leverage product data analytics to identify new service opportunities. For example, we were working with a consulting firm that specialized in optimization services for manufacturing and logistics companies. They created a software platform that collects data on how customers manage their inventory, logistics, and production lines. The software platform is equipped with sensors and AI algorithms that provide real-time analytics on operational efficiency, machine downtime, and workflow bottlenecks.

The product customer success team uses this data to proactively identify areas where clients may benefit from additional consulting services. If the analytics reveal consistent issues in a client's inventory turnover rates or production line efficiency, the customer success managers will work with the consulting team to initiate a conversation with the customer about targeted services such as additional training, process reengineering, or technology upgrades that could resolve identified issues.

Redefining success metrics to evaluate the performance of your bundled offerings is also critical. For example, the adoption rate of both products and services together or overall client satisfaction could both be additional performance measures for customer success in addition to traditional customer success metrics like product churn rates or customer lifetime value (more on customer success metrics in a minute).

Finally, the customer success function will need to adapt their renewal strategies to address the bundled nature of your offerings. For instance, you might notice that clients renew more frequently when they use both the product and the accompanying services, as opposed to using one or the other. Understanding these patterns allows for developing targeted strategies that enhance the value proposition over time, encouraging both renewals and expansions.

Retention Predictors

For your customer success function to identify customers at risk of nonrenewal early on, you'll need detailed usage data and churn rates to understand the usage patterns (e.g., levels and timing) that predict retention and the customer behavior that is likely to predict churn. Obviously, you won't have this information early in a product's maturity, but you should still make and document your assumptions about retention predictors (benchmarking data can be helpful here). As the product matures, these retention predictors can be validated and refined.

For example, usage metrics that indicate a customer is deriving value from a technology product could include logins, feature usage, data uploads, integrations setup, etc. Slack monitors the number of daily active users (DAU) within an organization. A high DAU indicates that the platform is essential for daily operations and communication, suggesting a healthy customer relationship. A drop in DAU can be an early warning sign of disengagement and potential nonrenewal.

As you get more data about usage levels and customer renewals, you can establish thresholds for healthy usage. As the product matures, these thresholds will likely differ by customer segment.

While you may track several key usage metrics, many companies find it useful to home in on "One Metric that Matters" (OMTM). The OMTM concept comes from Ben Yoskovitz's book, *Lean Analytics*, and it's the idea that even when tracking multiple metrics, there's one metric that we care about above all else. For example, one company included a live event as part of their product bundle and found that if a client attended the live event within the first three months of purchase, they were more likely to renew; therefore, live event attendance in the first three months was a good OMTM.

Slack also found that once a team collectively sends two thousand messages within the platform, they are much more likely to continue using the service actively and become long-term paying customers. Choosing and monitoring the right OMTM depends on understanding what drives value for your customers and aligning that with your product's strengths. Effective use of these metrics not only helps in predicting renewals but also in identifying areas to upsell or even services cross-sell.

Finally, usage data should be used to calculate and track a customer health score that aggregates multiple usage signals, qualitative feedback (from surveys, interviews, customer support interactions, etc.), expansion and upsell rates, and other engagement data points. This score can help segment customers into risk categories for prioritized action.

Organizing for Multiyear Deals

Multiyear deals are a strategic way to increase customer retention by securing long-term commitments from customers. From the customer perspective, multiyear contracts can reduce the hassle and uncertainty associated with annual renewal processes, and they are typically more cost-effective. This longer commitment period decreases the opportunities for customers to switch to competitors, fostering a more stable customer base and allowing deeper customer relationships to develop. Over the span of these contracts, you can better understand and meet the changing needs of your clients, really positioning your organization as a partner rather than a vendor.

However, multiyear deals also come with their challenges. Customers may hesitate to enter into long-term agreements, especially where technology evolves rapidly and/or business needs change quickly. There is a risk that a product may become less relevant over the contract duration, or that locked-in prices and terms might prevent a company from adapting to market dynamics. Moreover, if a customer becomes dissatisfied with the service, a multiyear contract can prolong the discontent, potentially leading to strained relationships and challenges once the contract is up for renewal.

Multiyear deals are a pricing and packaging strategy to consider once a product reaches a certain level of maturity. If a product is well-established and its benefits are clearly understood by a stable customer base, you can propose multiyear contracts more confidently.

You also have more confidence in your product economics and have a better sense of how a multiyear deal will impact profitability.

You will need to design appropriate pricing incentives for longer commitments which could include discounted pricing, locked-in rates (particularly appealing in industries where prices are volatile or rising), or additional features at no extra cost for the duration of the contract[69]. We especially recommend access to premium features, such as higher service levels, dedicated account management, or first access to new features and upgrades[70]. Another creative idea is to allow customers to add additional features at discounted rates when they lock in for multiple years or to provide early upgrade options for customers who sign multiyear contracts (i.e., customers can upgrade at a significant discount after two years within a three- or four-year contract). If you have a usage-based pricing model that scales with usage, you could also cap the maximum charge for customers in multiyear agreements. This cap provides cost predictability for customers managing large-scale operations and encourages them to engage in longer contracts for better budget control.

Another tactic that is very effective for services organizations that are productizing is to offer incentives or "loyalty credits" that customers can use for future product purchases or for services. These credits accumulate faster under multiyear contracts, encouraging longer commitments and increasing customer stickiness by offering tangible rewards for loyalty.

Key Takeaways

1. Managing the customer experience post-sales is one of the weaker areas for most professional services firms that are productizing and the *lowest* scoring area for all the go-to-market capabilities.

2. Most organizations *intend* for products to be renewable but don't properly *design* for renewal. And they wrongly think that if they create a subscription pricing schema, they will have recurring revenue. In fact, many B2B services organizations unintentionally design for churn instead of renewal from day one.

3. Product renewals require more dynamic monitoring of usage and ongoing product enhancements than in retainer-based services models. This includes a different set of customer health analytics, customer support, and engagement strategies.

4. We recommend investing in dedicated customer success before dedicated sales hires to ensure that new customers are onboarded effectively and that customers use and renew the offering.

5. For your customer success function to identify customers at risk of nonrenewal early on, you'll need detailed usage data and churn rates to understand the usage patterns (e.g., levels and timing) that predict retention and the customer behavior that is likely to predict churn.

6. If your go-to-market strategy includes bundling your products with services or even selling products alongside services, customer success and delivery teams need to be well-integrated.

7. Customer success can leverage product data analytics to identify new service opportunities.

Additional Resources

✗ Customer journey map

✗ Customer Success organization guidelines

✗ Sample Customer Success playbook

✘ Sample "what is account management?" training

✘ Recurring revenue product design checklist

✘ Customer health score template and survey questions

✘ One metric that matters examples

(Please download the tools at www.commercializebook.com)

CHAPTER 7

PRODUCT STRATEGY IS AT THE HEART OF SUCCESSFUL COMMERCIALIZATION

The most successful organizations will invest in the ecosystem of go-to-market capabilities to successfully launch more productized offerings—Market Understanding, Pricing and Packaging, Marketing, Sales and Renewability.

This starts when the organization finds an urgent and expensive problem that an attractive market segment has, and they design a **differentiated solution that customers will pay for over and over again.**

You can slap recurring revenue contracting terms on any offering, but the product needs to have recurring impact against an urgent and expensive problem. If you do not have this, you do not have a product business. This starts with making **product design** decisions that result in **high customer lifetime value**[*] rather than a services performance measure such as annual revenue.

As we mentioned at the beginning of this book, you are developing and fine-tuning your commercialization strategy throughout the entire cycle of market discovery, product design, development, launch, and management. Your product vision includes commercialization decisions, and your commercialization decisions will influence product design. This includes product design decisions such as how you will have recurring impact and how you will evolve the product beyond the MVP based on customer needs.

For example, when AMEND Consulting developed an industry-leading inventory optimization tool, its customers immediately wanted to put the tool into deployment. However, the AMEND team quickly found that using the tool required a higher degree of data integrity than most customers possessed at the time of onboarding. Instead of changing the tool to make it more friendly to data-poor environments—and thus depleting its value—they instead thought about the problem from a customer lifetime value lens.

AMEND restructured its customer journey around a solution package of services and technology that helped clients start from their current data environment and quickly grow its maturity to the point where inventory optimization through their AI tool was possible. Customers signed up for a three-year journey with a more predictable set of activities and predictable lifetime value.

---

[*]   Customer lifetime value predicts the total revenue a business can expect from a single customer account throughout the business relationship. It helps understand the long-term value of customers and the effectiveness of customer success efforts in retaining and upselling customers.

Product Design

Value Proposition Focused on Long-Term Value

Your product value proposition should clearly articulate how your product solves the specific urgent and expensive problems of your target market(s) over the long term. What is the recurring need, or what is the long-tail problem that the product solves? Part of this will be articulating how your product can grow and adapt with the customer's business and changing needs, as we discussed when designing packages that serve customers through different stages of maturity.

Recurring Impact

A lot of service organizations used to a project-based environment are wired to try and show as much value as soon as possible. But if a product delivers most of its value up front without ongoing additions or enhancements, customers may feel they no longer need to renew after they extract the initial value. This is common in software or content services where the newest features or content are highly touted at sign-up but do not evolve significantly over time.

Renewable products are designed, not just packaged and priced, to be renewable. For example, they should have recurring (and ideally, growing) impact over time. If your product doesn't have recurring impact, you won't earn recurring revenue.

The best recurring revenue products create more value the more customers use it. This could be because as you get more intelligence and information about the customer, the product gets better at serving them. Most products that leverage AI have this as a key part of the value proposition.

One example of recurring impact is customer data platforms, such as Segment and Tealium, that collect and unify customer data across multiple touchpoints. With increased usage, these platforms can offer deeper insights into customer behavior, enabling more personalized marketing and sales strategies. As more data is integrated, the accuracy and effectiveness of the segmentation, targeting, and personalization improve, making these tools increasingly valuable. Another example is AI-driven supply chain management tools like Llamasoft (now part of Coupa) and ClearMetal, which use machine-learning algorithms that improve with more data. These tools analyze historical supply chain data to forecast demand, manage inventory, and optimize logistics. The more data these tools process, the better they become at predicting disruptions and suggesting efficient routes and inventory levels, thus becoming more valuable to the user[71].

Or it could be that the customer is also able to leverage more features as they become more mature in using the product. A classic example of this is HubSpot's Marketing Hub. When customers first adopt it, they typically leverage basic features like email marketing and lead capture forms. However, as their marketing operations mature, they can unlock greater value by utilizing HubSpot's more advanced capabilities such as marketing automation, content management, social media management, ad management, and revenue attribution reporting.

Not Stopping at the MVP

Organizations that are successful at productizing commit to continuing to develop and evolve their products after launch. This is hard for organizations not used to staffing post-launch teams to make a product better. But you need the capacity to measure what you learned from the MVP launch, develop new hypotheses about the next stage of growth, and use reserve investment dollars and people to improve the product.

Products should be regularly updated and improved based on customer feedback, new information, competitor enhancements, and technological advancements. This is especially true if underlying base data is part of the product such as regulatory laws, standards, or market conditions that can change quickly. If customers find the product's underlying data unreliable, they will not renew.

Investing in User Analytics and Customer Feedback Collection

Without data on who, how, and when a product is being used, it is hard to understand the usage patterns that lead to renewal or churn.

The product either must be designed to capture user data, including who, when, and what was used or you need to leverage a class of software like Pendo, Walkme, Heap, etc. that offer analytics, guided product walk-throughs, and feedback capture. It's a rapidly evolving field that's getting faster to deploy and adding more AI to bring forward customer usage insights more quickly.

Not only does customer usage data serve as a leading indicator as to whether a customer is likely to continue to buy or not, but it also tells us why. To understand why a product is performing well (or not so well), we need to create a plan to test our original hypotheses about the product and not just look at the performance of certain product features. For example, why does the customer use the product? How do they use it? What benefits do they receive from it? Original product hypotheses (along with ease of use and overall customer satisfaction) should be regularly evaluated.

Use a mix of quantitative analysis (e.g., product usage data, customer data, etc.) and qualitative research (such as win/loss analysis) to evaluate how many sales opportunities are won or lost and why. In addition, twice-a-year customer surveys or customer advisory board feedback can be helpful. Analyzing product usage data by customer segments is very important, which is why data analysis is a valuable skill in any product manager's toolbox.

✗ Unit economics calculation template

(Please download the tool at www.commercializebook.com)

Orienting Around Customer Lifetime Value

Rather than focusing on traditional measures such as annual revenue, gross margin, and net profit, to successfully plan for renewals from day one, you'll need to change the organization's focus to customer lifetime value.

Customer lifetime value is influenced by measures such as:

1. Churn rate (the percentage of customers who stop using the product or service over a given term),

2. Renewal rate (percentage of customers who renew their contracts or subscriptions at the end of a term),

3. Net revenue retention (percentage of recurring revenue retained from current customers over a specific term, including upgrades, downgrades, and churn).

Shifting the focus to customer lifetime value can be challenging if your historical focus has been on winning contracts and delivering on them effectively. For starters, many B2B services firms lack the necessary data systems to track and analyze customer interactions throughout their life cycle effectively. As we discussed in chapter 5, adjusting performance metrics and incentives is crucial. Rewarding delivery teams not just for the sales they close but also for the ongoing satisfaction and retention of their clients can change behavior.

Conclusion

Our hope is that after reading this book, you have the confidence you need and the tools you require to successfully make decisions about your organization's strategy to successfully commercialize your more productized offerings. Decisions about who you will sell to, how best to monetize your innovations, and how to market, sell, and renew are fundamental to your success, and your answers to these decisions will evolve as your offerings mature and you learn more about the market.

The best way to learn more will not be through months and months of research. It will be through putting fear aside, putting something in the market for prospective customers to react to, learning, and evolving. The concepts we've outlined, the stories we've shared, and the tools on the website *www.commercializebook.com* should provide the basics to get you started.

We also highly recommend assessing your own organization's commercialization readiness by taking a quick assessment at *https://www.vecteris.com/commercializationreadinessassessment*. This proprietary assessment will help you better understand you're the strengths and weaknesses of your organization's go-to-market capabilities for your productized offerings. Revisit the assessment as often as you like to track your progress and identify new areas of focus.

Also, don't be afraid to ask for help. We and the rest of our colleagues at Vecteris have extensive experience transforming services to be sold as products. We're here if you need the support.

ACKNOWLEDGMENTS

Thank you!

The entire team at Vecteris thanks the hundreds of CEOs, executives, and product professionals who have used our services, joined our peer groups, participated in our training programs, and used our tools to support their productization journeys. You've helped us live our mission to help organizations design and launch forward-thinking products to positively impact the world.

Several of these leaders and companies shared experiences and perspective that contributed to this book. Thank you to Greg Alexander, Matthew Ansbro, Michelle Anthony, Andy Armstrong, Rob Cybulski, Matt Dixon, Anthony Donatelli, Russell Dumas, Sarah Eppler, Simon Frewer, Andrea Fryear, Whitney Gibson, Kate Gruelich, Jay Hampton, Darren Horwitz, Kristen Howe, Brian Joseph, Mike Jozwik, Jeff Kleinschmidt, Brian Lee, Ted McKenna, TA Mitchell, Allen Mueller, Matt Murphy, Samantha Polovina, John Riley, Caroline Ritter, Heather Ryan, Paul Saville-King, Heather Schimmel, Bobby Smyth, Katie Trauth Taylor, Rich Wagner, Ed Walton, Ajay Wanchoo and Alex Yastrebenetsky.

You generously shared your stories and lessons learned so that we might all benefit.

The Team

No book comes into existence without a talented team of writers, editors, researchers, marketers, and designers. To Jaime Drennan, Molly Connolly, JeiLi Merrill, Lauri Hershner, Nicole Merill, Calvin Armstrong, Arjun Gupta, and Colin Froehle.

To Ann Thompson, Christoffer Ellehuus, Jennifer McCollum, and Sue Baggott, you go above and beyond in your roles as advisors. Your belief in us fuels us, and your wise counsel helps us course correct and grow.

Eisha's Acknowledgments

To my family, thank you for letting me be me. I love you.

Thank you to all the women in my life who cheered me on while I worked on this, especially Maureen D'Angelo, Kristen Pung, Shannon Keesee, Beth Driehaus, Susan Jackson, Mymy Ha, Lori Aronson, Lessa Trindle, Kelli Stein, Annabel Tierney and my soul sisters Heather Tierney, Nicole Ferry, and Sarah Brown.

To my clients who have become dear friends and encourage me to keep sharing my gifts, especially Kristen Howe, Stacey Bain, Brian Joseph, Leela Wilson, Craig Todd, Jeff Spanbauer, Bobby Smyth, Paul Delaney, David Veile, Geoff Marsh, Michael O'Brien, and Nancy Aichholz.

To those who have supported our own productization, especially Jim Salters, John Handelsman, and Chad Mattix.

Jason's Acknowledgments

To Lauren, you keep us ever moving toward the horizon. To Zella, our greatest mission in life.

To my community of friends, mentors, customers, and partners— our ongoing dialogues keep right action tethered to great thinking. In particular, Eisha Armstrong, Dan Herd, Tim Raiswell, Bryan Kurey, Scott Engler, Craig Risberg, Christoffer Ellehuus, Marita Hansen, Matt Stone, Chris Morris, Gray Hunter, Jerrod McCarty, Casey Bolton, Jack Compton, David Evans, Elenie Panos, Jay Carnes, Jonathan Knoth, and so many more.

Sean's Acknowledgments

To my wife, Carrie Gillispie, for being my partner in all things. Thank you for your intelligence, humor, great questions, your voice, and for loving me for exactly who I am.

To my children, Evan and Hannah, for bringing so much joy, laughter, and wonder into my world. I do it all for you.

To my parents and my brother and sister for being constant cheerleaders and forcing me to take some moments to appreciate and celebrate my accomplishments.

To my friends, I am so blessed that there are too many of you to list. Know that each one of you brings me joy, and I feel it is a privilege to be part of your lives, have fun together, support each other, and just generally share experiences. I cherish them all.

To my mentors, colleagues, clients, both past and present, every one of you has been an invaluable teacher and influence along the way. I am in constant awe of each person's unique perspectives, skills, and personal flair you bring to your work. I am beyond lucky that many of you have become friends.

ABOUT THE AUTHORS

Eisha Armstrong is the executive chairman and cofounder of Vecteris, where she works with B2B services companies around the globe on new product strategy and commercialization. She has over twenty-five years of experience developing, launching, and managing new data and information service products. Prior to cofounding Vecteris, Eisha held senior product leadership positions both with E. W. Scripps, the diversified media company, and with CEB (now Gartner), the world's largest  membership-based corporate performance research and advisory company. Eisha earned her MBA at the Harvard Business School and her bachelor of arts in both women's studies and economics at the University of Kansas. She is also a certified yoga teacher, and she believes that teaching yoga makes her a better leader.

Jason Boldt is Vecteris's chief growth officer. He has over a decade of experience building, launching, and scaling B2B information services and SaaS products. He spent a decade at CEB, now Gartner, where he oversaw new business and product launches, led international expansion, and served as an advisor to C-suite clients. Most recently, he was a commercial leader at WorkBoard, a high-growth Series D B2B SaaS company. Jason has a dual MBA from Columbia Business School and London Business School and a BS in financial economics from Centre College.

Sean Gillispie is a product coach at Vecteris, where he works with B2B services organizations to successfully launch new product offerings. He has over twenty years of experience delivering innovative products as a strategic product leader, entrepreneur, and management consultant. Prior to Vecteris, Sean held senior product management and strategy positions for several B2B SaaS organizations, including as VP of product at Employee Navigator, head of product at CultureIQ, director of product at CEB Workforce Surveys & Analytics, and director of strategic programs at Social Solutions. Sean co-founded and successfully sold Stratasense, which delivered groundbreaking in-site PV solar testing solutions. Sean holds an MBA from Babson College, and a BA in computer science from Williams College.

ENDNOTES

Preface

1 Eisfeldt, Andrea L, et al. "Generative AI and Firm Values." National Bureau of Economic Research, May 2023. *https://www.nber.org/papers/w31222.*

2 O-Shea, Catherine, Kara Uchtman, and Katie Trauth Taylor. "Generative AI Storytelling for Innovative Enterprises." Generative AI Storytelling for Innovative Enterprises, April 2023. *https://www.narratize.com/.*

Chapter 1

3 Sheehan, Mary. The Pocket Guide to Product Launches Get Confident, Go to Market, and Win. La Vergne: Houndstooth Press, 10, 2023.

4 Content Capital. "Helping You Determine the Best Path Forward for Your Content." Content Capital. *https://sterlingwoods.com/blog/selling-professional-services/.*

5 Van Der Kooij, Jacco. Essay. In How to Get $10M in ARR and Beyond, 15, 2019.

6 Armstrong, Eisha, Jaime Drennan, and Molly Tipps. Fearless: How to transform a services culture and successfully productize. Cincinnati, OH: Vecteris, 153-157, 2023.

7   Gillispie, Sean. "2024 Productization Benchmarking Report." Cincinnati, 2024.

8   Blundell, Richard, Paul Watson, and Chris Tottman. The Go To Market Handbook for B2B SaaS Leaders. Axelerants Limited, 156-157, 2023.

9   Gillispie, Sean. "2024 Productization Benchmarking Report." Cincinnati, 2024.

10   Van Der Kooij, Jacco. Essay. In How to Get $10M in ARR and Beyond, 14, 2019.

Chapter 2

11   Ulwick, Tony. "The Jobs-to-be-Done Growth Strategy Matrix." Medium. Last modified January 5, 2017. *https://jobs-to-be-done.com/the-jobs-to-be-done-growth-strategy-matrix-426e3d5ff86e.*

12   Walling, Rob. Story. In The SaaS Playbook: Build a Multimillion-Dollar Startup Without Venture Capital, 63, n.d.

Chapter 3

13   Lehrskov-Schmidt, Ulrik. The Pricing Roadmap How to Design B2B SaaS Pricing Models That Your Customers Will Love. La Vergne: Houndstooth Press, 35, 2023.

14   Lehrskov-Schmidt, Ulrik. The Pricing Roadmap How to Design B2B SaaS Pricing Models That Your Customers Will Love. La Vergne: Houndstooth Press, 26, 2023.

15   Walling, Rob. Story. In The SaaS Playbook: Build a Multimillion-Dollar Startup Without Venture Capital, 52-53, n.d.

16   Lehrskov-Schmidt, Ulrik. The Pricing Roadmap How to Design B2B SaaS Pricing Models That Your Customers Will Love. La Vergne: Houndstooth Press, 19, 2023.

17   Lehrskov-Schmidt, Ulrik. The Pricing Roadmap How to Design B2B SaaS Pricing Models That Your Customers Will Love. La Vergne: Houndstooth Press, 41, 2023.

18   Lehrskov-Schmidt, Ulrik. The Pricing Roadmap How to Design B2B SaaS Pricing Models That Your Customers Will Love. La Vergne: Houndstooth Press, 35, 2023.

19   Lehrskov-Schmidt, Ulrik. The Pricing Roadmap How to Design B2B SaaS Pricing Models That Your Customers Will Love. La Vergne: Houndstooth Press, 157, 2023.

20   Blundell, Richard, Paul Watson, and Chris Tottman. The Go To Market Handbook for B2B SaaS Leaders. Axelerants Limited, 2023.

21   Blundell, Richard, Paul Watson, and Chris Tottman. The Go To Market Handbook for B2B SaaS Leaders. Axelerants Limited, 203, 2023.

22   Blundell, Richard, Paul Watson, and Chris Tottman. The Go To Market Handbook for B2B SaaS Leaders. Axelerants Limited, 206, 2023.

23   Cision US. "Miller Heiman Group Launches Sales Analytics Platform Linked to Major Methodology Update." PR Newswire. Last modified July 10, 2018. *https://www.prnewswire.com/news-releases/ miller-heiman-group-launches-sales-analytics-platform-linked-to-major-methodology-update-300678221.html.*

24   Lehrskov-Schmidt, Ulrik. The Pricing Roadmap How to Design B2B SaaS Pricing Models That Your Customers Will Love. La Vergne: Houndstooth Press, 80, 2023.

25   Bush, Wes. Product-led Growth: How to Build a Product That Sells Itself. Waterloo: Product-Led Institute, 108, 2019.

26   Bush, Wes. Product-led Growth: How to Build a Product That Sells Itself. Waterloo: Product-Led Institute, 75-76, 2019.

27   Walling, Rob. Story. In The SaaS Playbook: Build a Multimillion-Dollar Startup Without Venture Capital, 84, n.d.

28   Lehrskov-Schmidt, Ulrik. The Pricing Roadmap How to Design B2B SaaS Pricing Models That Your Customers Will Love. La Vergne: Houndstooth Press, 127, 2023.

29   Ellis, Sean. "Product/Market Fit Survey by Sean Ellis and Gopractice." Product/Market fit survey by Sean Ellis and GoPractice, 2023. *https://pmfsurvey.com/.*

30   Van Der Kooij, Jacco. Essay. In How to Get $10M in ARR and Beyond, 29, 2019.

31   Essay. In The Pricing Roadmap: How to Design B2B SaaS Pricing Models That Your Customers Will Love, 251–53, 2023.

Chapter 4

32   Becker, John. "Marcus Sheridan: They Ask, You Answer Is a Business Philosophy, Not a Marketing Strategy." IMPACT, December 10, 2021. *https://www.impactplus.com/blog/they-ask-you-answer-is-not-a-marketing-strategy*.

33   Sheehan, Mary. The Pocket Guide to Product Launches Get Confident, Go to Market, and Win. La Vergne: Houndstooth Press, 89, 2023.

34   Blundell, Richard, Paul Watson, and Chris Tottman. The Go To Market Handbook for B2B SaaS Leaders. Axelerants Limited, 43, 2023.

35   Blundell, Richard, Paul Watson, and Chris Tottman. The Go To Market Handbook for B2B SaaS Leaders. Axelerants Limited, 40-43, 2023.

36   Zak, Paul J. "Why Your Brain Loves Good Storytelling." Harvard Business Review. Last modified October 28, 2014. *https://hbr.org/2014/10/why-your-brain-loves-good-storytelling*.

37   *https://www.lusha.com/blog/b2b-lead-conversion-rates-benchmarks/*

38   *https://www.swordandthescript.com/2023/10/b2b-marketing-budget-as-a-percentage-of-revenue/*

39   Walling, Rob. Story. In The SaaS Playbook: Build a Multimillion-Dollar Startup Without Venture Capital, 103, n.d.

40   Gartner. "Gartner Predicts Search Engine Volume Will Drop 25% by 2026, Due to AI Chatbots and Other Virtual Agents." Gartner. Last modified February 19, 2024. *https://www.gartner.com/en/newsroom/press-releases/2024-02-19-gartner-predicts-search-engine-volume-will-drop-25-percent-by-2026-due-to-ai-chatbots-and-other-virtual-agents*.

41   Neumann, Nico, Catherine E. Tucker, Kumar Subramanyam, and John Marshall. 2023."Is first- or third-party audience data more effective for reaching the 'right' customers? The case of IT decision-makers." *https://hdl.handle.net/1721.1/152922.*

42   Bush, Wes. Product-led Growth: How to Build a Product That Sells Itself. Waterloo: Product-Led Institute, 31, 2019.

43   Walling, Rob. Story. In The SaaS Playbook: Build a Multimillion-Dollar Startup Without Venture Capital, 97, n.d.

44   "What is AWS Marketplace?" Amazon Web Services. *https://docs.aws.amazon.com/marketplace/latest/buyerguide/what-is-marketplace.html.*

45   *https://www.linkedin.com/pulse/perfect-b2b-website-service-page-13-point-checklist-andy-crestodina-1c/*

46   Blundell, Richard, Paul Watson, and Chris Tottman. The Go To Market Handbook for B2B SaaS Leaders. Axelerants Limited, 135, 2023.

47   Howley, Carol. "Council Post: How to Navigate the Changing Customer Buying Journey." Forbes, February 8, 2023.

48   Ellis, Sean, and Morgan Brown. Hacking Growth. N.p.: Random House, 44, 2017.

49   Sheehan, Mary. The Pocket Guide to Product Launches Get Confident, Go to Market, and Win. La Vergne: Houndstooth Press, 132, 2023.

50   Conant, Latané. No Forms, No Spam, No Cold Calls: the Next Generation of Account-based Sales and Marketing. Hoboken, NJ: John Wiley & Sons, 98, 2023.

51   *https://hbr.org/2023/04/the-rebirth-of-software-as-a-service.*

52   Verna, Elena. "Elena's Growth Scoop: Elena Verna." Substack, 2019. *https://elenaverna.substack.com/.*

53   Bush, Wes. Product-led Growth: How to Build a Product That Sells Itself. Waterloo: Product-Led Institute, 37, 2019.

54   Bush, Wes. Product-led Growth: How to Build a Product That Sells Itself. Waterloo: Product-Led Institute, 28, 2019.

55 Bussgang, Jeffrey, and Oliver Jay. "How Software Companies Can Avoid the Trap of Product-Led Growth." Harvard Business Review. Last modified September 22, 2023.

56 Bush, Wes. Product-led Growth: How to Build a Product That Sells Itself. Waterloo: Product-Led Institute, 30, 2019.

57 Bush, Wes. Product-led Growth: How to Build a Product That Sells Itself. Waterloo: Product-Led Institute, 111-118, 2019.

Chapter 5

58 Armstrong, Eisha, Jaime Drennan, and Molly Tipps. Fearless: How to transform a services culture and successfully productize. Cincinnati, OH: Vecteris, 174, 2023.

59 Blundell, Richard, Paul Watson, and Chris Tottman. The Go To Market Handbook for B2B SaaS Leaders. Axelerants Limited, 164-167, 2023.

60 Van Der Kooij, Jacco. Essay. In How to Get $10M in ARR and Beyond, 25-27, 2019.

61 Blundell, Richard, Paul Watson, and Chris Tottman. The Go To Market Handbook for B2B SaaS Leaders. Axelerants Limited, 170-172, 2023.

62 Van Der Kooij, Jacco. Essay. In How to Get $10M in ARR and Beyond, 76-81, 2019.

63 "What Today's Rainmakers Do Differently." Harvard Business Review, January 16, 2024. *https://hbr.org/2023/11/what-todays-rainmakers-do-differently.*

64 Armstrong, Eisha, Jaime Drennan, and Molly Tipps. Fearless: How to transform a services culture and successfully productize. Cincinnati, OH: Vecteris, 83, 2023.

65 Stefanie Faupel and Stefan Süß, "The Effect of Transformational Leadership on Employees During Organizational Change – An Empirical Analysis," Journal of Change Management 19, no. 3 (March 13, 2018): 145-166, *https://doi.org/10.1080/14697017.2018.1447006.*

66 Blundell, Richard, Paul Watson, and Chris Tottman. The Go To Market Handbook for B2B SaaS Leaders. Axelerants Limited, 164-165, 2023.

Chapter 6

67 Cespedes, Frank V., and Jacco van der Kooij. "The Rebirth of Software as a Service." Harvard Business Review. Last modified April 18, 2023. *https://hbr.org/2023/04/the-rebirth-of-software-as-a-service.*

68 Fontanella, Clint. "The Beginner's Guide to Building a Successful Customer Success Program." HubSpot Blog, June 15, 2021. *https://blog.hubspot.com/service/customer-success-program.*

69 Kooij, Jacco van der. "How to Create a Go-to-Market Strategy with Our Proven Template." GTMnow, August 20, 2023. *https://gtmnow.com/go-to-market-strategy/.*

70 "Reasons to Consider a Multi-Year SAAS Contract." Vertice, February 21, 2024. *https://www.vertice.one/inside-saas/multi-year-saas-contract.*

Chapter 7

71 Cencioni, Paolo, Jacopo Gibertini, David Sprengel, and Martina Yanni. "Next-Gen B2B Sales: How Three Game Changers Grabbed the Opportunity." McKinsey & Company, March 12, 2024. *https://www.mckinsey.com/capabilities/growth-marketing-and-sales/our-insights/next-gen-b2b-sales-how-three-game-changers-grabbed-the-opportunity.*

GET STARTED NOW to develop and commercialize your productized offerings.

Download 30+ actionable *Commercialization* tools.

Complete our *Commercialization Readiness Assessment* to assess key GTM gaps for your productized offering.

Vecteris' Productize Pathway® Solution enables you to develop and commercialize productized offerings.

B2B Services organizations partner with us to:

DEVELOP	COMMERCIALIZE	TRANSFORM
• Validate offerings with attractive market potential	• Validate pricing, packaging, and sales channel for target market	• Roadmap required capabilities for productization
• Assess the feasibility and roadmap for productizing	• Develop sales & marketing capabilities for productized offerings	• Structure teams and processes across product and GTM
• Accelerate time to market and iteration	• Align GTM incentives, skills and processes	• Operate a product-centric organization and culture

 Productize Pathway® Solution

For a fraction of the cost of an FTE, unlock your team's capabilities through:

- Unmetered, Dedicated Productization Coaching
- Product MVP and Pricing & Packaging Accelerators
- Facilitated Workshops and Organizational Keynotes

- Product and Commercialization Assessments and Benchmarks
- Executive, Product and Commercial Leader Peer Groups
- Vecteris Knowledge Hub Platform

©2024 Vecteris